D0862980

A Look at Life *from a* Deer Stand

Steve Chapman

HARVEST HOUSE PUBLISHERS
EUGENE, OREGON

Illustrations © Steve Chapman

Cover photo © Charles J. Alsheimer

Cover design by Koechel Peterson & Associates, Inc., Minneapolis, Minnesota

A LOOK AT LIFE FROM A DEER STAND
Copyright © 1998, 2012 by Steve Chapman
Published 2012 by Harvest House Publishers
Eugene, Oregon 97402
www.harvesthousepublishers.com

ISBN 978-0-7369-7168-3 (Milano Softone™)
ISBN 978-0-7369-4896-8 (pbk.)
ISBN 978-0-7369-4898-2 (eBook)

Library of Congress Cataloging-in-Publication Data
Chapman, Steve.
 A look at life from a deer stand / Steve Chapman.
  p. cm.
 Originally published: Madison, TN : S&A Family, Inc.; 1996.
 ISBN 978-1-56507-864-2
 1. White-tailed deer hunting—Anecdotes—Tennessee. 2. Conduct of life—Anecdotes.
 3. Chapman, Steve. I. Title.
 SK301.C514 1998
 799.2'7652'092—DC21

                                        97-42832
                                        CIP

Printed in China

      17 18 19 20 21 22 23 24 25 / RDS-SK / 10 9 8 7 6 5 4 3 2 1

My dedication and thanks for giving me a reason to write this book go to the following folks in my life:

- To P.J. and Lillian Chapman, my parents, for trusting me in my younger years with an activity that has its dangers.

- To Kenneth Bledsoe for taking me on my first hunt in 1964.

- To Annie, my wife, for "making me" go to the woods from time to precious time.

- And to my arrows, Nathan and Heidi, for keeping me straight.

Contents

Foreword

In many ways I knew Steve Chapman before I ever met him. In 1985 I became acquainted with his music. I'll never forget the first time I heard Steve and Annie sing their popular song "Turn Your Heart Toward Home". Its message to the families of America is powerful, and to this day I find myself humming the song and thinking about its words. I've since become a big fan of Steve and Annie Chapman's music.

Though our careers are much different, Steve and I have several common bonds that draw us together. Certainly our love for the family and the joy we share in knowing Jesus Christ as our Savior are paramount. However, the thing that caused us to finally meet and become friends was our mutual love and respect for the white-tailed deer. Not long ago we spent an afternoon kicking around our farm, looking at whitetails and talking about deer hunting. Steve's made a name for himself with his music, but I don't know if I've ever met a more avid whitetail hunter. The mere mention of whitetails puts a smile on his face and a twinkle in his eye.

So when Steve asked me to write the foreword for this book, I was more than curious (and excited) about what the book would be like. His title intrigued me and, knowing his gift for writing, I was anxious to see the manuscript. Suffice it to say, I couldn't put it down. I was struck by Steve's unique and wonderful way of communicating his deer-hunting experiences and his outlook on life. At times I found myself roaring with laughter. Other times I sat thinking about the serious side of his words…words that vividly illustrate how I can become a better person, a better father, a better husband… the things that matter most in life. He makes me think. The man is a breath of fresh air, a living and breathing gift from God. Blending "down-home" (or should I say "backwoods"?) humor and candor, Steve has masterfully written down many of the things we as hunters think about while sitting on a deer stand.

You're in for a real treat. But be forewarned: This is not your typical deer-hunting book. No, it will not tell you how to kill the biggest buck in the woods. But it might change your life. It is a powerful work from one of the country's top songwriters. When I finished the last page of the manuscript, I gazed out the window and pondered what I had just read. Over and over one thought kept coming back to me: *A Look at Life from a Deer Stand* should be mandatory reading for every deer hunter in America. It's that good!

Charles J. Alsheimer
Field Editor, *Deer and Deer Hunting*

Introduction

The dry, fallen leaves lightly crunched on the ground behind the tree I was perched in, and my heart started to race. I knew that sound. It was not a squirrel or a busy chipmunk stirring back there. The sound was unique. I had heard it before. I didn't move a muscle, even though everything within me wanted to shift my body to take a look. I fought my instincts and sat motionless, gripping my compound bow in my nervous hand and rehearsing the steps to pull to a full draw.

It seemed like an hour before I heard the next step, though I knew that less than a minute had passed. These situations always make life seem longer. I turned my eyes in their sockets as far right as I could and hoped for movement. Sure enough, I saw a form move and then stop. As slowly as a shadow on a sundial, I rotated my head and looked down. Eighteen feet below my treestand stood the creature I had been waiting for. It was an eight-point white-tailed buck deer. What a rush!

My wait to spot such a magnificent creature had not begun that morning 30 minutes before daylight. Instead, my vigil started the day hunting season had ended the year before. I was, to put it honestly, addicted to the rush of excitement I felt in that moment.

Getting close enough to hear the cautious footsteps of one of the smartest animals on the earth is absolutely intoxicating. Add to that ingredient an attempt to inflict the animal with a fatal wound using a primitive weapon like a bow and arrow, and you have the makings of adrenaline pie. I was loving it!

That morning, the unsuspecting buck moved about five more yards ahead and was then beyond my tree. His body language told me that he was not unusually cautious. He was being his normal careful self. That signified to me that he didn't know I was there. He intermittently looked on down the ridge and then dropped his head to search the forest floor for acorns.

I had done some thorough preseason scouting and figured he would pass on my left where the trail was. I am a right-handed shooter, so I set up to accommodate my type of shot. However, years of experience had taught me one sure thing: It's impossible to consistently predict a deer's movement, and you can never be totally certain about his habits. This buck was proving me right. Because of my position, I had to make some adjustments before I could shoot my bow. I had to stand and shift my entire body slightly to the right, which involved the risk of being detected. I knew that anything could happen—from my treestand squeaking to my hat falling off. I had no choice, however. I had to stand up.

With every ounce of control I could summon, I tightened my already-tense leg muscles and slowly, yet quietly, began to stand up. I moved only when the deer's head was behind a tree, concealing his eyes. My legs trembled some as I stood, but it didn't surprise me. I had dealt with this before. I knew the challenge of "buck fever." This level of excitement has been known to cause heart attacks in some hunters. Why should a little trembling of the body not be expected? Finally, I was standing. So far, so good!

The buck had not seen me, and I watched him take a few more casual steps. He was about six feet right of my 20-yard yellow ribbon marker that I had hung from the branch of a sapling. It was an ideal distance for my ability. I quietly connected my mechanical release to the string and waited for the right moment to raise my bow to a drawing position. I also reminded myself that white was the color of the 20-yard pin mounted to my sights.

With my stance finally in position, my upper body was about to be put to the test. My arms and back muscles had to pull the string back, which was set at 63 pounds pull weight. As pumped as I was, one would think it would feel like 63 ounces. Not so! In that scenario, it felt as if I were pulling back on a tightly wound piano string. I couldn't believe how my arms shook as I attempted full draw. It had been much easier back on the practice range. I felt embarrassed at how hard it was.

As if being instructed by an outdoor-magazine photographer, the eight-point turned broadside as I searched for him in my peep sight. *This is too easy,* I thought. I lined up the white pin on his vital area and began the slight finger pressure on the trigger of the release. *Stop!* The target moved. He took three large steps and suddenly was standing behind a large oak. All I could see was his head and his rear. His vitals were protected by a ton of the hardest timber in the woods. I held at full draw another 20 to 30 seconds and finally succumbed to the loss of strength.

As I let the bow limbs relax, something awful happened. The aluminum arrow that was sliding across the vinyl-coated prongs of the rest somehow jumped out and banged against the riser of the bow. The metal-on-metal "click" sound that it made would hardly have been noticeable on the practice range, but in the woods it sounded like the crack of a baseball bat at Wrigley Field. The buck immediately detected the source of the noise, and the white warning flag went up. The dirt flew as he dug into the soft ground under the leaves, and as quickly as he had come, he was gone. Also missing were some valuable possessions of mine like pride, ego, happiness, and confidence. I was hurt!

Though the buck ran off and left me frustrated and disappointed, he didn't take with him my ability to learn. As a result of that morning, I now have mounted on the riser of my bow a patch of soft, self-adhesive moleskin material—the type one uses to doctor their feet. I at least was able to add one more important lesson to the long list of dos and don'ts required to be successful in taking a whitetail. Experience is indeed the best teacher.

Such is deer hunting. Every time I walk into the woods, I learn something new. It really is one of the joys of the activity. While some people would be absolutely bored out of their minds sitting for hours hoping to get close to a deer, I find that it is full of fathomless fun. Unlike the pilot that said, "Flying is hours and hours of boredom interrupted by moments of stark fear," deer hunting is hours and hours of sweet anticipation graced with moments of incredible excitement.

Though it may be difficult at times to justify an activity not necessary for most of us in this modern age, there are some practical benefits that can be enjoyed from hunting the whitetail. For example, venison is a wonderful food source. I readily admit that meat for the table is much cheaper (and more easily obtained) at the local market. My wife, Annie, has calculated that the cost of venison can range from 5 dollars a pound for a local deer in Tennessee to 13 dollars per pound for a western deer. Of course, my response—and I'm sure you've used this argument at one time or another—is that the meat is lean and good for the heart.

Another helpful contribution to many of us is the needed break from our busy lifestyles that hunting provides. The mental medicine is very effective and comes much less expensively than what one can get on the psychiatrist's couch.

Besides the healthy meat and the healing therapy of simply being in the wild, there is one other benefit I have gleaned from deer hunting. I call it the "harvest of truths." While it's a fact that each time I go out I learn something new about a hunting tactic or a technical improvement to my equipment, there are greater lessons about life that I have "bagged" that are now mounted on the wall of my heart. These trophies are a result of the "think time" that hunting yields. Those hours of waiting were never wasted as I sat and observed the nature that surrounded me and studied the process of hunting. Some amazing parallels between what happens in the woods and what takes place in life have been discovered during those hours of silence. For example, on the morning described above, I found that my equipment needed certain adjustments to function more effectively. In the same way, I have come upon needed changes in my life that have made me better equipped to accomplish other tasks. Areas like being a husband and father, or a laborer and a friend have needed slight "tuning" from time to time. The pages that follow are a collection of these discoveries, as well as some modifications in my life that came about because of the valuable lessons I learned from being a hunter.

I have a feeling that if you are a hunter too, some of the "truths" I have found while hunting deer will be familiar. Perhaps there are some life-altering lessons you have drawn from being in the woods that I am yet to apply. (Just give me time!) If you're not a woodsman or woodsperson, this writing may still interest you because there is so much to learn "out there." So, come along. Let's go hunting and we'll take a look at life from a deer stand.

1

First to Last

Have you ever noticed that there is something about "firsts" that intrigues us all? We find ourselves spellbound by them, and for some reason we focus on them and often refer to firsts as the highlights of our lives. Consider the importance we place on the following:

Firstborn
First step
First word ever spoken
First grade
First date
First kiss
"First time ever I saw your face"
First car I ever owned
First man on the moon
First cup of coffee
First impression

On and on the list could go. As I pondered our affection for firsts, I began to realize that we are drawn to these initial events because they seem to have a unique ability to set the course for the journeys we take, whether good or bad.

In my 30-plus years of avid hunting, I still look back at my first morning in the woods as my most favorite outdoor experience. To this day I truly believe it put me on a path which I hope to travel as long as I'm able to get around. Maybe you have a fond memory of a similar experience that set you on the same course.

For me, the journey began when I was 14 years old. My dad was pastor of a church in the rolling hills of West Virginia, and among the members of his congregation was a gentleman named Kenneth Bledsoe. One Sunday after the service, he invited me to join him on a squirrel hunt the following Saturday. I could hardly wait for the end of the week to come. Finally, Friday came and my folks took me to his home. It sat along a rural highway on top of a ridge surrounded by gently rolling hills. His land was graced with large patches of woods and beautiful meadows. It was the middle of October and all the leaves on the trees were ablaze with incredible autumn colors. The red, brown, orange, and yellow hues seemed to glow in the bright sun with an invitation to simply stand in awe of God's ability to paint a scene. The view that spread out before us was like a huge canvas, and we were fortunate to be living creatures on it.

I went to bed that night and quickly drifted off into a deep slumber. Little did I know that from that evening on, I would never go to sleep so easily on the night before a hunt. For the rest of my life, the anticipation of a repeat of the morning to follow would always make me anxious for the alarm to sound.

At 5:30 A.M. we were sitting down and having breakfast. It hadn't happened often that I was up at that hour. Perhaps Easter sunrise service or leaving early to drive with my folks to Grandma's house were the only reasons you would find me up before daylight. But there I was, wide-awake with anticipation and already dressed for the day.

In the dim light of the carport, Kenneth handed me the gun he had shown me how to use the night before. It was a .22/20 gauge over and under masterpiece. He put a half dozen 20-gauge shells in my hand, and we walked across the paved road at the end of his driveway and headed down a hillside into the darkness of the woods. My friend knew his way very well through the forest. Nearly every step of the way, he gave me instructions that would ensure our safety. When we came to the first fence, he held out his hand to take my gun. He said, "Never cross a fence while holding your gun. Too many guys have died that way." Also, he warned me about choosing my steps carefully in the dark. He said, "Falling with a gun is no fun, especially for those around you!"

I was getting my first safety course that day, and I felt secure with such a veteran hunter as Kenneth. I couldn't have chosen a better teacher. Many times throughout my hunting life, I have applied the lessons I learned that morning. Years later, when I finally did take an official hunter's safety course here in Tennessee with my son, I was amazed at how much ground had already been covered by my friend who had never seen the textbook. Someone had taught him well, and I was grateful that the heritage was handed down to me.

About 20 minutes before daylight, we stopped by a large oak. Kenneth took his foot and with his big boot he scraped away the dry leaves on the forest floor to reveal an area of dark, soft ground about three feet wide and three feet long. He said softly, "You'll need a quiet place to sit. You don't want to be making a lot of noise while you hunt. You're in the critters' territory. They know sounds. Unfamiliar noises are a sign of danger to them. Now, have a seat here and try to move only when it's time to take a shot." Then, as if I were being left on a deserted island, he walked up the hill behind me and out of sight. Just before he left, he whispered, "I'll be around the hill. Stay here till I come back and get you."

It was the next 30 to 40 minutes that forever sealed the joy of hunting in my heart. There I sat, outside, under a tree as the world came to life. Creatures began to respond to the rays of the sun that crept over the top of the ridge. With each passing minute, an excitement started to build inside me. I heard all kinds of sounds I had never heard before. Crows were cawing in the distance, speaking an unknown language. Leaves were mysteriously rustling on the ground somewhere nearby, a hoot owl made its call, and an amazing variety of birds began to sing their tunes. Like a city going to work, the animals that didn't work the night shift (like raccoons and possums) began their foraging for food. It was absolutely amazing to me that such a kingdom existed and that I was sitting in the middle of it.

All my five senses seemed heightened that first morning. The wonderful taste of an early breakfast of eggs, bacon, toast, and jam that Evelyn Bledsoe had prepared still lingered on my tongue. The crisp, cool October air felt refreshing on my skin. The scene of the growing light made me grateful for eyesight, and my hearing was experiencing a virtual orchestra of new sounds. For a young city slicker, I found the experience brought a sense of great joy. For some odd reason, however, the fifth of the senses that was blessed seemed to be the one I remember the most. It was the incredible smell of the autumn woods. There is no other aroma like it in the world. There's no way to explain it. To this day, the smell of the forest floor triggers more memories and a stronger desire to head to the woods than any of the other senses.

An hour must have passed as I sat there. I never did see a squirrel. Perhaps I shifted around more than I should have and scared them off. Also, it's possible that a dozen squirrels may have scurried right above me in the canopy of branches and I just didn't see them. I was still sitting in my quiet spot that Kenneth had prepared for me at the base of the tree when suddenly I got a tap on the shoulder. It made a shiver race up my spine that took years to go away. It's a wonder I didn't fire the gun I was holding across my lap. I quickly turned around to see the bear before it ate me and felt greatly relieved to see it was Kenneth standing there. He saw what he had done to me and chuckled as he softly said, "The hunt is over."

"How did you do that? I never heard you coming!" I said in much too loud a voice for the great hunter.

He simply whispered, "I can teach you to do that." And so he did. On the way back to the house, he began to teach me the art of stalking through the woods. He showed me how to pick a place void of fallen twigs, put the toe down first, and then set the rest of the foot down gently. He instructed me to not forget to stop often and keep the eyes moving like radar across the woods. The techniques I gleaned from his seasoned wisdom that morning have yielded some impressive mounts that hang on my walls today.

That first morning in the woods opened a door to a whole new world and left pleasant and permanent tracks in my memory. When you think about your initial hunt, there's a lot more to it than one has time to share. Yet, all who hunt will cherish the "first," and it will always hold its rightful place in your thoughts. I know this is true, because there is a head mount hanging over our son's fireplace. It's a white-tailed deer. The six-point rack is not large, but the plaque beneath it makes it a huge deer. It reads, "Nathan's First Deer."

My first deer had even a smaller rack, but was nonetheless important. I had it mounted, and it still brings just as much joy as the six-by-six elk rack I brought home from Montana. The memory is as sweet. I'll never forget that day. Not only did I enjoy taking my first whitetail, but there were other firsts that I treasure.

For example, my very first ride in a four-wheel-drive vehicle took place the morning of my first deer hunt. It was frightening, but I survived it. The driver was an elderly gentleman whose flame was fueled by the fear in his passengers. He seemed to be intoxicated by the challenge of getting that olive-green used Army-issue jeep up that steep West Virginia mountain. I repented of every sin I could think of, and even started in on the sins of my friends as we bounced up "death road."

Another first I experienced that day is what is known as a "drive." It's a hunting tactic used most often in the later part of the season to push the deer out of the dense brush into the open woods by driving them with a line of hunters walking through the thickets. A deer usually heads for the low gaps in the ridgeline called a "saddle," and that's where I was standing when I took my first shot at a buck. What an incredible moment it was. It's as exciting to think about it now as it was when it happened. If it's a memory you share, you understand the rush of feelings I can still remember years later.

Also, with the help of my host, Max Groves, I gutted a deer for the first time. (I should say "field dressed" the deer for those who are squeamish.) It's a disgusting but necessary process.

That wonderful day ended with another first. Mrs. Groves prepared the evening meal using venison that I had "harvested." It was a gastronomical jubilee! She panfried the backstrap and then made a gravy to pour over it. She graced the tender meat with mashed potatoes, green beans, corn, hot yeast rolls, and a steaming pot of fresh-brewed coffee. (If you can, please try not to drool on these pages.)

It is true that we humans are enamored with firsts. However, as wonderful as they are, I do have one problem with them. The fact that there are firsts indicates that there will come a last. A beginning represents an ending that must follow. It would be hard to number how many mid-morning departures from a deer stand I have dreaded to make. With a reluctance that tempts me to forsake all other responsibilities, many times I have stood up, gathered my gear, and headed to the truck. I often whisper to myself as I'm walking away, "All good things must end!" As much as I would like to be able to, I can't keep the curtain from falling on a great day afield.

Life is a lot like a day in the woods. It has a beginning and an end. We take the alpha with the omega. The firstborn will leave home. Someday there'll be a final step. There'll be a last kiss, a last word, a graduation, a good-bye, a sunset, and—brace yourself—there'll even be a last hunt. When will it be? Who knows?

What we do with all that is between the crib and the casket is an awesome opportunity and an incredible responsibility. Maybe some of us have deviated from the course that had a great and worthy beginning. Maybe we have forgotten our "first love." Perhaps some of us have given so much attention to other interests that we have forgotten how much we would enjoy an autumn sunrise or a quiet November deer stand. How easy it is to get caught up in the cares of this life and forget to go "outside."

For some of us, there are other things besides hunting that had a wonderful and true beginning but, because of various distractions, we have forgotten how to enjoy them. For example, how long has it been since we enjoyed a date with a spouse that resembles the first date? What about those first hours with a new baby? Have we hugged our children like that since? Perhaps a friendship needs to be rekindled. For some of us, maybe it's been a long time since we communed with our Father in heaven the way we did when we first gave our lives to Him.

May I suggest that you stop for a moment and take in a deep breath? In the way that the smell of an autumn morning brings back the precious memory of a first hunt, perhaps you could catch the aroma of another part of life that had a wonderful beginning. I pray that if you do, you will once again enjoy it. May you do so before time slips up behind you, taps you on the shoulder, and says, "The hunt is over."

SC 95

2

The Ultimate Sacrifice

If you are a serious hunter like me, I know you have come to understand the word *sacrifice*. The list of things one must give up in order to fill the big game tag attached to a hunting license is significant. Yet, because of the thrill of a challenge, deer hunters press on and willingly pay the price. It's a form of rigid self-discipline that has its rewards. However, a problem can arise when other people are pulled into the river of our sacrifices.

I vividly recall one hunt when I was a teenager that two gentlemen had a right to regret. It involved the father and a brother of the girl I would eventually marry. I met Annie in 1963 in junior high school. I was 13 years old and she was 12. (It was love at first sight— for Annie!) Later on, at 16 and 15 years of age, we were in different grades, but we did share one class together: the school choir.

One November day in the chorus room, Annie began telling me about the deer her brother had taken on her dad's farm. When I perked up, she was delighted. Little did I know that she had a "crush" on me, and that my immediate interest in the deer story was possibly a key that could unlock love's door. She hinted that I might be welcome to hunt on the farm, so I seized the moment and asked her if her brother might be willing to put me in the stand where he had experienced success. Annie responded with a cautious yes. Not wanting to miss a golden opportunity, I set a time to be there and spent the rest of the week dreaming about the upcoming hunt.

Sleep is definitely high on the list of things that hunters sacrifice. When the next Saturday finally came, the alarm roused me from my warm bed at 2:30 A.M., and I was out the door and on my way to the Williamson farm by 3:30. The real reason for my early departure was I was afraid I wouldn't be able to find their farm in the predawn darkness. And it would have been tragic to have missed such a grand hunting opportunity. Therefore, giving up my sleep in order to arrive there at the right time seemed the safe thing to do. As it turned out, I drove up their lane around 3:45 A.M. Not wanting to disturb anyone that early, I sat in the car for a few moments trying to decide whether or not to go to the front door. Everything seemed so calm. I hated to be a bother. I was hoping a light would come on and signal me that they were aware of my presence. Still, no one stirred.

Being driven, however, by the prospects of a large buck passing under that treestand, I cast aside politeness, exited the car, and walked up to the porch and approached the door. I gave it an old-fashioned knuckle knock. Nothing happened. I waited a few cold minutes, then tried again. No response. I rapped one more time with vigor and—aha!—the lights snapped on. About a minute later I heard the locks turn from the inside. The door slowly opened to reveal an older man who I assumed was Annie's father. He looked a little bewildered and rather concerned.

Feeling pretty awkward, I quickly introduced myself and felt relieved to see him put the pieces together and realize that I was Annie's guest. I said, "Annie told me that your son has agreed to take me to his favorite treestand this morning. I sure do appreciate it, and I'm ready to go." He gave me a "Do-you-know-how-early-it-is?" look and then said, "Have a seat and I'll get my son up."

In a few minutes a younger man came into the living room. He seemed like the quiet type, and was rubbing his eyes. He simply said,

"Let's go." Justifiably so, Annie's brother was not too pleased to partake in my sacrifices and, regretfully, in all my excitement to "bag" a big one, I was unable to detect his suffering.

Comfort is another item that hunters trade for the taste of venison. Annie's dad had briefly given up a warm bed to answer the door. However, his son and I were about to make a greater sacrifice. The temperature was around 15 degrees, and the windchill put it in a dangerously frigid range. Any sweat we worked up as we trudged along in silence immediately froze on our clothing. Our lungs also paid a price as we climbed the hill toward the ridge. We had left the house around 4 A.M., and by 4:30 we were standing at the base of the tree looking up at the stand. After making sure that I had safely climbed the wooden steps that were nailed to the forks of the tree and was standing securely on the plywood platform, my host left me in the dark. As I watched the dancing beam of his flashlight disappear into the distance, I had no idea that I was about to face a near-death experience.

Being somewhat naive in my career as an outdoorsman, I had not yet learned the effectiveness of layering my clothes. When I had tumbled out of bed that morning, I had thrown on one of the thickest sweatshirts I could find, two pairs of pants, a coat, and a pair of my dad's thin work gloves.

In those days, blaze orange had not yet been introduced to the hunting community, so hunters wore reds and other bright colors. I knew that safety was a factor, so I did the best I could. I borrowed my dad's yellow rain suit, which fit loosely over my clothing, and at least I felt safer. However, I had not counted on one problem. The frigid air made the plastic brittle, and every time I moved I sounded like breaking glass, so I had to remain as motionless as possible. Consequently, the warming effect of moving around could not be enjoyed and I quickly became quite cold and miserable. The frightening thing was that it was around 5 A.M., nearly two hours before daylight.

Time had literally frozen too. It came to a standstill because the cheap watch I was wearing had stopped working around 4:40 A.M. It just couldn't operate in such cold weather. As a result, the encouragement that came from checking the time and anxiously awaiting the sun's first rays was sadly lost.

As the pain began to set in, I thought about abandoning my treestand and leaving. It was only 5:30 A.M. (I guessed.) However, I couldn't do it. I didn't dare take the risk of the Williamsons seeing me drive away and turning their sacrifices into a worthless effort. Also, I couldn't go back to the car, start it up, get warm, and then return to the stand. I knew I would never be able to find it again. I was stuck.

I wiggled my toes and fingers inside my boots and gloves. I tried flexing different muscles and then relaxing them to create some movement in order to warm myself. Nothing seemed to work. Very simply, I was freezing to death. All my burial would require would be to melt me and pour me into a jar. After all these years, I have never experienced a more painful battle with cold weather than I was having that morning.

I'm not sure how I survived to see it happen, but finally the sun began to peek over the ridge. It was a welcome sight. Around 6:45 (I guessed) I was standing in a spotlight of sun rays. Even though it was slight, I could feel their warmth. It gave me enough hope to press on. By 7:30 (I guessed) I was able to think rationally once again, and I began to recall my purpose for being there. Suddenly, I heard a twig snap. I could feel the adrenaline start to flow, and a bead of perspiration formed on my brow. This was it!

Somehow I knew the twin brother to the buck Annie's brother had taken was coming up the ridgeline. Slowly, I felt for the hammer of the lever action 30-30 that I gripped in my hands. As I prepared for a shot, I mentally began to rehearse the speech I would give at the local hunting club, since I would probably receive the award for the biggest rack. Suddenly, out of the mist came the source of the noise. Walking right up to my treestand, my "trophy" looked up at

me and said, "Seen anything this morning? Sorry to bother ya!...
Guess I'll be going now...."

What a brutal addition to the discomfort I had endured already!
As the unwelcome intruder crunched away in the frozen leaves, I
honestly thought of firing a few angry rounds at his feet just to watch
him dance. Instead, I exercised self-control and simply wished that
the fleas of a thousand camels would infest his hunting coat.

My sacrifice of sleep and comfort yielded nothing that cold and
miserable day in the way of table meat. What's worse, I had involved
others in the losses. I will forever appreciate Annie's brother's willingness to guide me that cold morning to the treestand. But I will
always regret appearing so selfish as to arrive at such an ungodly
hour on a day so bitterly cold that even the watchdogs were not
fools enough to leave their warm beds to bark at my car as I drove
up the driveway.

The inconveniences and discomfort that I put my future in-laws
through that morning years ago were significant. However, they are
smallscale when compared to the sacrifices I have been known to
require of those now closest to me. I speak of my wife and children.
Through time and tears I have thankfully learned that it is unwise
and dangerous to drag them into an unbridled and relentless pursuit of the whitetail. If I'm not careful to keep things in balance, I
will drown out their appreciation and approval of my interest in
hunting.

How many of us have knowingly left behind "deer widows and
orphans" for the sake of a hunt? Have we, in our untamed enthusi-
asm for a close encounter with a whitetail, allowed our families to
experience the loss of emotional rest, mental comfort, precious time
with their husband and father (or wife and mother), and even the
loss of limited financial resources? It is indeed a temptation that is
hard to resist. Perhaps some of us, however, have felt the bitter-cold
wind of the potential loneliness that would result and have awakened in time to the need to make that critical adjustment to our

outdoor lifestyles. Those who have done so know that it is not, by any means, an easy change to make.

I have decided that my wife and children are much more important than any animal, or any fish, or a golf ball, a job, or any other pursuit that would require too much of their lives. By the grace of God, this hunter has come to grips with the fact that while getting close to a whitetail buck is an incredible challenge (which I enjoy with a passion), a much greater challenge is to see how far away from a deer I can get when I realize that pursuing it is costing my family too much. For a hunter, that is the ultimate sacrifice.

SC
95

3

The Arrow and the Bow

I really didn't mind that by the time I reached the stand of trees and set up my portable treestand, I was in a drenching sweat. I was happy just to be on that wooded hillside in Cheatham County, Tennessee. At that time in my life, I was a novice bowhunter. I immediately was consumed by it. I knew very little but wanted to learn it all. So I spent days—even weeks—getting ready for the season. I loved every part of it—even the sweat. I had a pawnshop Bear Whitetail compound bow and some arrows I had found at a garage sale.

At the time our children were very young. In fact, one was "in the oven." Heidi was due in a few months, and Nathan was not yet three years old. I'm not sure how many children it takes to fill the proverbial quiver, but ours was full with two. I am very grateful for them and love them both with all of my heart. Early on in my fatherhood, I had a strong desire to be the best dad I could be, but I couldn't see a mistake I was making. I was allowing my new interest in archery to threaten the time and attention that belonged to my children.

Sitting in that treestand, I waited from sunup till about 9:30 A.M. There was no movement, no noise—just dead silence. I was having a problem staying awake. I know I dozed off several times. In fact, during one snooze that probably lasted 30 seconds but seemed like an hour, I found myself dreaming. When I opened my eyes, all I could see was the ground about 20 feet below. I thought I was falling, and it startled me to the point I gasped loudly. I immediately realized where I was and began to laugh.

I needed a way to stay awake, so I took the opportunity to check out my equipment. The compound bow cams, cables, grip, sights, silencers, and the broadhead tip all seemed to be in order. I then eyed the arrow for straightness, and that's when a phrase passed through my head. It sounded so good in my thoughts that I said it out loud: "the arrow and the bow." Somehow it sounded melodic to me, more so than "bow and arrow." As a songwriter, I'm always considering how words are metered together, and this phrase grabbed my attention. I thought to myself, "I'd like to use those words in a song someday."

The woods continued to be totally silent, and the humidity made it feel like I was sitting in a steam room. Under my camo head net, the sweat poured off my forehead and into my eyes. Another annoying challenge to my concentration were the pesky little gnats and mosquitoes that made that high-pitched buzz around my ears and swarmed menacingly around my eyes. I hate that. Every time I deal with those disgusting pests, I have to say, "Thanks, Adam! These nasty creatures are a product of sin!"

Wishing for more enjoyable thoughts, my attention went back to that phrase "the arrow and the bow." I began to ponder the meaning, and a sobering analogy came to mind. *The bow is like the parent and the arrow is like the child.* A flood of thoughts followed. First, there will come a day when I'll have to let my children go. Just like I draw back the arrow and release it at the right moment, so it should be that I release my children at the right time. I don't look forward to that day, but if things go normally, they'll eventually leave. The "drawing back" starts early in their lives. Second, at what target am I aiming my arrows? If I want their lives to be placed in the center of

God's will, then that's where I must aim. What am I doing to help make it so?

Also, am I as the bow rightly tuned and in good working order? And in whose hands am I? Furthermore, am I really willing to let go? I once heard of some parents who learned that their son desired to go to a foreign mission field. Out of fear for their own welfare and a selfish clinging to the child, they manipulated the situation and blocked the response to the call which God had placed on that young heart. The child eventually chose a vocation unrelated to the mission field. As his feelings of failure and resentment grew, his spiritual life took a dangerous turn. Only then did his parents realize what a terrible mistake they had made to discourage the child from entering the ministry. They were overwrought with regret. I don't want to be guilty of standing in the Lord's way when it comes to His desire for my children's lives. I must be willing to release them to His call. He knows what's best for their lives. Besides, who knows how many lives will be touched with the gospel through our children? There's a saying that states, "You can count the seeds in an apple, but you can't count the apples in a seed." So it is true that we can count the kids in our house, but we'll never know how many children of God will be added to His family as a result of our kids' devotion to Christ.

Also, will I do well at letting them go to another's love? I think of my sweet Heidi. It's going to be tough to let her go to some young twit. Excuse me. I mean some young man. I agree with whoever said, "Giving your daughter away in marriage is like giving a fine, priceless violin to a gorilla!" I don't look forward to the day when the question is asked, "Who gives this bride away?" I hope I am sensible in that moment.

But I must let go. It wouldn't be fair to my arrows to keep them protected in a quiver. To make that mistake would prevent them from fulfilling their purpose. The following is a lyric that was born that morning in my treestand.

The Arrow and the Bow

Here is wisdom for the moms and dads
That time has proven true
The day your children learn to walk
They start to walk away from you.

For at first you hold all of them
Cradled safely in your arms
Then one day their hand is all you'll hold
Then soon it's just their heart.

And there'll even come the time
If your love for them is true
You'll have to let their hearts go free
To let them love
Someone else not only you.

Can the sparrow ever learn to fly
If the nest is all it knows?
Can the arrow ever reach its mark
By remaining in the bow?
You have to let it go.

Here is wisdom for the moms and dads
That time has proven true
The day your children learn to walk
They start to walk away from you.[1]

Now my children are older, and fortunately I did listen to better judgment. I backed off in the amount of time I was spending in the field, and instead of losing a closeness to my son, he has now become my hunting buddy. Whenever I buy new equipment, I have to purchase it in pairs, and I do so with pleasure. I also hunt with Heidi, by the way. Her game, however, is a little different. Let's put it this way: Nathan likes to wear hunting clothes; Heidi likes hunting for clothes. The "neat" part of Heidi's hunt is that the game is already hanging and cleaned when we shoot it.

The Arrow and the Bow

To close, may I suggest a prayer for fathers who hunt:

Oh, Father in heaven
Make me to be a fine-tuned bow in Your hands.
Use my life to make the arrows You have given me
    to fly accurately and confidently to the
    destination You have chosen.
Help me to bend well under the tension of parenting.
And someday, should that incredible miracle happen,
    and You turn my arrows into bows,
    may they too understand the act of letting go.
In Jesus' name, amen.

4

The Doing of This Thing

The following letter appears in a book by my wife, Annie, and me titled *Married Lovers/Married Friends* (Bethany House Publishers, Minneapolis, MN). From a father in Michigan, the letter reads:

> During your concert, I determined to spend the next day, Saturday, with my children, ages six, three, and one and a half. I was up building block houses much earlier than I expected, and by 10 A.M. we were still going strong. My 18-month-old son was about to knock down my six-year-old son's castle. Instead of shutting him out of the fun behind a gate, I swooped up my 18-month-old and twirled him around the room. It was at that moment my wife walked in and informed me that my son, who was sitting on my head, had a load in his pants that was dripping into my hair. My nose said, "She's not lying." So I passed him to my wife, jumped in the shower, turned on the water, and found only cold water due to my wife doing loads of laundry that morning. As I stood there freezing, I wondered, "Is this the family fun you spoke about the night before?"

This letter goes to prove that spending time with your children has its risks. Yet, that father is to be commended for his fine effort.

I am confident that his children will not forget the fun. (His barber won't either!) It's true there may be painful results from being close to the kids. Every time I look in a mirror, I see the scar on my face from the five iron golf club I let my daughter swing years ago. Yet, believe me, the bond that results far outweighs all the risks involved.

There are as many ways to spend valuable time with children as there are children to spend time with. The possibilities are endless! From bicycle rides to building a dollhouse together, from going to a concert to stopping by the yogurt shop, or simply taking them with you to the hardware store. For some of us, taking a kid to the woods is a great way to build the parent/child relationship.

I had been doing just that with my son, Nathan. He had accompanied me during the late-fall and early-winter gun seasons, but I remember the day I discovered an item that could broaden the time frame that we could hunt together.

I stopped by a local pawnshop to see if they might have a good used climbing treestand that some frustrated hunter might have traded in for an item less treacherous. As I looked around, I spotted a nice compound bow that looked quite new. It was a late-model bow, and it seemed to be the perfect thing I could use to entice my son into joining me in archery season. The bargain price made it irresistible, so I bought it and took it home. I equipped it with a used set of sight pins, a new peep sight, silencers, and a "hand-me-down" release. Nathan's interest in the art of archery quickly grew. He spent a lot of time practicing, and soon became rather proficient. His "groupings" at the target were impressive.

As bow season drew near, I detected a reservation in Nathan to hunt so early in the year. After some probing, I discovered why he preferred entering the woods on colder days. His hesitancy about going on a late-September bow hunt was largely due to his serious hatred of spiders. (I tell this with his permission.) Here in Tennessee, any hunter who hunts early in the season must brave horrible encounters with webs large enough to catch bull elk. I share my son's disdain for these creatures. There have been times when I would be scouting in late summer for a place to put a stand, get onto a good deer trail, put my eyes to the ground, and unknowingly walk into one of these "traps." If someone were standing by with a video camera, they would get remarkable footage that would ensure them an appearance on "America's Funniest Home Videos." The very second I feel a web wrap me up, I start my "spider dance." Sort of a jig. I whip off my hat, flap my arms vigorously, and mutter unintelligible words. I'm sure I look like someone involved in some sort of tribal dance. So I did understand Nathan's resistance to venturing into the woods during archery season. He would rather wait until after a frost or two. However, the anticipation of getting his first deer with bow and arrow proved too much for a born hunter to pass up.

The night before the September 30 hunt, I talked him into going with me by assuring him I would bravely lead the way to his stand and clear the path of any spider webs.

The next morning greeted us with a cool 65-degree temperature. Hoping that all the spiders were hiding from the chill, I "cut" our way through to the ladder stand I had set up over two converging deer trails. I gave Nathan last-minute instructions to wait in the stand until I came back to him. If he had not seen anything after a few hours, perhaps my movement through the woods would drive a deer by him. I hurried to my stand in a race against daybreak. As I walked along at a brisk pace, I prayed that no spider(s) would drop down into his lap or encompass him in a disgusting web if he drifted off to sleep. I knew that if a "close encounter" occurred, our hunt would be over in a flash. The high-decibel scream he would let go would scare everything away for miles around.

I finally settled into my stand about daylight and began the wait. Around 8:00 A.M., a large doe came within range. I slowly pulled back, took careful aim, and let the arrow fly. I meant to hit the doe, but I honestly didn't see the tree I killed. That baby weighed in at around 2000 pounds field dressed. I was devastated and embarrassed, even though no one was around to witness the errant shot. I thought my hunt was over, but at 8:30 two more deer came by. I took aim and pushed the release button, sending the arrow on its way. I missed the deer but I killed the earth. Yes, sir! I hit it dead center! It weighed in at 6000 billion billion tons. I thought about having it mounted, but I couldn't drag it home.

I couldn't believe it. Two shots in 30 minutes, and all I had to show for it was a dead tree and a fatally wounded planet. I felt even worse when I realized I had used a 20-yard pin for a 15-yard shot. Plus, shaking like Barney Fife didn't help much either.

I began to wonder how Nathan was doing with all the training I had given him. I had coached him as he spent several hours popping a 3D target and plugging a bag full of old rags. He took shots from every angle and his accuracy was quite good, but in no way could I prepare him to deal with the kind of disappointment his dad was feeling that morning. I should have told him that it's easy to pick a spot on a 3D target because it doesn't move. However, when that target has real fur and looks right at you with those big brown eyes, you do well to remember to breathe. I shook my head and wondered if Nathan had the chance to "blow it" the way I had already done. I started feeling sorry for him.

My two stray arrows hurt even worse because I had been trying for so long to fill an archery deer tag. It's tough to admit, but when I'm standing in a treestand looking at a whitetail with its ears and tail perked up, it does strange things to my ability to concentrate. Consequently, the years had ticked away with no tangible results. I kept telling myself it was no big deal, but I wasn't listening. It was a painful morning.

As promised, I headed back toward Nathan's stand about 9:00 A.M. I didn't want to hurry through the woods. Instead, I wanted to move slowly enough to cause any deer that might move in front of me to do so in a walk and not a run. So I eased along as quietly as I could.

I knew I was about 200 yards from Nathan when I came near a little rise. Suddenly, two deer that were bedded down stood up about 20 yards away. I was behind some brush with the wind in my face. The two deer just stood there trying to figure out what I was. They each lowered their head, then quickly popped back up to see if I would move. Somehow I managed to remain motionless on the outside. On the inside, however, I was quivering like Jell-O on a jackhammer. Amazingly, they both took a few steps and simultaneously stepped behind trees that concealed me from their eyes. I raised my bow and pulled back. As I came to full draw, the thought came to me, *Three shots in one morning? This can't be true! No pressure now because no one would believe this anyway!* The one on the left, a young buck, had moved into the clear and was looking down the hill. I let the arrow go and heard the "thud" that occurs when an arrow connects. By then my heart was pounding and I was breathing hard. I dropped my bow to my side and listened. I could hear the crashing, and I had a feeling Nathan did, too.

The deer bolted over the rise and out of sight. I waited four or five minutes, then walked over to the spot where my arrow had found its mark. I followed the trail of freshly disturbed ground for just a few yards and immediately found blood. I knew this was a day I would never forget—my first deer with a bow. I waited ten more minutes before continuing, then found a serious blood trail. After a few more yards, I decided to turn around and head for the truck and let the deer lie down. I circled another way back to the pickup where I would leave my gear and then go to Nathan.

When I got to the truck, I couldn't believe my eyes. What I saw was unbelievable. Nathan was standing over a huge doe he had arrowed around 8:15 A.M. It was his first bow hunt and his first full draw at a live deer. I had heard of these kinds of beginner stories, but only in far-off hunting grounds. But here was an actual tale waiting to be told.

Nathan got even more excited when I told him I had a deer

down, for he knew it was my first as well. We stood there on that warm September morning basking in the glow of the turn of events. To make the memory even more special, when I later tracked my animal to its final resting place, I discovered that both deer had lain down about ten yards apart.

We must have told each other the story 20 times that day. And each time we recalled something new. I'm sure we'll tell it many more times, and with each rendition the deer will get bigger, the shots longer, and my two errant arrows will sink further into the "leaves" of forgetfulness.

I'm glad I've been able to make these kinds of memories with Nathan. Our hunting experiences have provided some great father/son time. From the teaching of the safety rules of firing a weapon to the sound of the alarm clock that wakes us up on the first morning of season, we have gathered much to talk about.

One of the best benefits of our time together is the door of conversation that is opened as a result of the "doing of this thing." It has led to other subjects that are of greater importance than hunting. We've talked about girls, the Bible, politics, technology, girls, sports, aviation, girls, family, future, and girls, to name a few subjects.

It seems that most moms feel comfortable to simply sit and talk with a child. Moms don't have to be pounding nails, or casting a spinner bait, or building a rocket to feel at ease in conversation. As a result, they make great listeners. Many dads, however, like to do and talk. At least it's true for me. Maybe you're that way, too. Somehow the "distraction of action" creates an environment for men to communicate. But whatever it takes, dads need to talk to their kids.

I once saw a quip that said, "A child needs his father's presence more than his presents." How true. In order to create those times of togetherness, hardly anything works better than a mutual involvement in a sport. There are times when a dad has to be willing to sacrifice his own enjoyment of an activity in order to build a young child's interest in it. I realized early in my experience as a father that, for example, if I wanted to be with my kids, I could take them fishing. But if I wanted to go fishing, I didn't take the kids. Fishing can be very risky with little ones. I advise you to keep a pair of needle-nose pliers and a first-aid kit in the tackle box.

Because I started hunting with my son when he was very young, and gave up a few shots of my own, being in the woods in the pursuit of big game has grown into a wonderful way to be together for us now. But whether you're a Daniel Boone dad or a Daniel Webster dad, it's not too late for you to find something fun to do with your child. It's important to ask ourselves the question, "What would keep me from planning a family camping trip, a bike ride with a son, a walk with a daughter, or a dinner and a decent movie with just the kids?" What could possibly be more important than the benefits of quality time with your children?

My dad always said, "People do what they want to do!" As a pastor who always hoped for folks to want to be in church, he prayed that their "want to" would change. Psalm 37:4 is a familiar favorite passage that states, "He will give you the desires of your heart." It's not just the object of the desire that God wishes to grant, but instead He wants to replace an old desire with a new and improved one. When it comes to dealing with the conflict of interests that steals our presence from our children's lives, we should sincerely pray and ask God to change our desires. Though the "tug" is strong to do that which we want to do, we must let a change in our "want to" take place.

Perhaps there is a dad, like yourself, who is wishing for a change of heart and determining even now to spend some needed time with his children. Please don't let anything rob your ambition. Go ahead and take the risk. It won't hurt too badly. I promise. Just keep in mind that during your time together someone just might say the words "I love you."

Man to Man

You were four years old but it wasn't too soon
First time we said ladies please step out of the room
Your Mama and your sister seemed to understand
You and me had to talk man to man.

When they closed the door we opened our hearts
Had a serious talk about Matchbox cars
It was a day I will never forget
We had a moment and it's not over yet,

Talkin' man to man
Heart to heart
It's kept this father and son
From drifting apart
And I know we'll always be close
No matter where we are
'Cause we've been man enough to talk
Heart to heart.

Sometimes we were kings
Talking issues of the world
Sometimes just two fellows talking 'bout girls
And those November nights we'd make our plans
Two great white hunters talkin' man to man.

Now it'll come too quickly
It'll come too soon
When again we're saying ladies
Please step out of the room
Your Mama and your sister and your bride to be
They'll know the moment's just for you and me

Talkin' man to man
Heart to heart
It's kept this father and son

From drifting apart
And I know we'll always be close
No matter where we are
'Cause we've been man enough to talk
Heart to heart.

And someday when the years go by
And I come to see you and what I find

Is a little boy who looks just like you and me
And he calls you "Daddy" will you promise me?

That you'll talk man to man
Heart to heart
It'll keep a father and son from drifting apart
And I know you'll always be close no matter where you are
'Cause you'll be man enough to talk heart to heart.[2]

A special thanks to the following families who have helped me make some great hunting memories with my son: the Bledsoes, the Williamsons, the Richeys, the Zehners, the Stearns, the Goodmans, the Jahns, the Pickards, the Thompsons, the Stoners, and the Petrichs.

5

He's Comin', Daddy

When we pulled up in front of the rustic-looking cabin, the first thing I noticed was its matchbox size. It wasn't much larger than the pickup we were in. I noted that there were no electric wires running to a pole nearby. It meant that there would be no convenience of an electric stove and no after-dinner TV that evening. Somehow, though, it didn't matter. My son and I, along with two other fellows, were there to hunt deer. So what if we didn't have an inside toilet or running water. So what if our refrigerator was a cooler and a bag of melting ice and that we would be sleeping head-to-toe. That was part of the fun! Getting ready for the sack by the light of a Coleman lantern was pure adventure. "Bring on the primitive lifestyle!" we declared. "We're men!" (Besides, in less than 48 hours we knew we would be on our way back to an easy chair in front of a fire!)

This was the fourth year for Nathan, my son, to go after his first elusive whitetail. The property we were going to hunt on was leased by a group of gentlemen who had formed a hunting club, and we were there as guests. Their choice of territory revealed their understanding of the deer's ideal habitat. The mountainside was covered with huge hickories and oaks. The woods were mostly clear and open, yet edged with inviting thickets for cover. It looked like a place that deer dream about. It held great prospects for Nathan's success that year.

I had suspended my pursuit of deer for the previous three years to help Nathan. We first went through the Hunter's Safety Course together. I highly recommend it, and think it very wise to require youngsters to take it. It best teaches the most important element of hunting—*safety*. Even adults can benefit from the course.

We then shopped for a good gun that best suited the region we would hunt most, as well as a caliber that Nathan could handle at his young age. We settled on a 30-30 lever action. That gun came in his second season. The first year he hunted, he carried an old .12-gauge single shot and "slugs." His move to a high-powered rifle was, to say the least, an exciting event for him.

For a total of three years, we faithfully trekked into the woods together in various places with no yield of venison. "This year," we thought, "it's gonna be different."

The alarm went off at 4 A.M. and hurt my slumbering ears on that first of two mornings we would hunt. We had to be on our way at 4:30. The walk would take 45 minutes or more…uphill all the way.

After breakfast we set out at a careful pace. It was dark and slow-going. Fortunately, our host had a four-wheeler and could carry our packs with dry clothes to the top. We were left to carry our heavy guns up some steep terrain. Before long my lungs were burning as the path kept turning sharply up…and up. We weren't prepared for this kind of pain.

At one point, Nathan stopped and bent over double with his face near the ground. The fellow we were climbing with said, "Nathan, are you OK?"

"Yes…" he huffed. "I'm just checking the leaves!"

For the rest of the trip we each used that line more than once, accompanied by a chuckle.

Drenched with sweat, we finally reached the top, as dawn began to lighten the sky. As we changed clothes in the cold November air, we did the "chill-bump cha-cha." We also were dancing a little to ease the leg cramps caused by the climb. A pitiful sight!

Nathan and I took a westerly route into a wooded section. We had never been on the property, so at random I chose a place for us to sit as daylight gave more distinct form to the trees and valleys beneath us. After an hour I left Nathan sitting and walked around a little to check things out.

I found a few tracks along a possible run. But the morning passed with no gunfire. I returned to Nathan, and we walked back to a designated spot on the ridge for a noon snack with the other two hunters.

Eating is one of our favorite things to do during a hunt. No food is off-limits in the wild. All concern about fat grams, cholesterol, and calories is cast aside. Somehow we talk ourselves into believing that we burn it all off during the hunt. I don't think my "caloric calculations" would support what we want to believe. My average deer-hunt lunch probably has about 87 grams of fat and 7028 calories. As for "burn-off," the average deer hunt probably accounts for only 822 calories and burns maybe 2.3 grams of fat. These are, of course, my estimates but are probably close to accurate, give or take a thousand calories or so.

Soon lunch was over and it was time to return to the stands and fight the "sugar blues." (Not to fear, we each had a Butterfinger bar we could inject intravenously at about 3 P.M.) I returned with Nathan to the area we had hunted that morning and sat with him on a flat facing north. The day was getting on, and we had not seen even the flick of a whitetail to speak of. About 2:30 I instructed him to stay there till I returned, and I again went to check out the surrounding area. This time, I discovered some serious deer signs. Three well-worked scrapes and some rubs gave away what I thought to be a buck's territory. I made some mental notes on how to find the place again. Right about dark, I returned to Nathan. He looked glum. I felt the same.

The whole day had passed without even an opportunity to feel the heart race. Tomorrow was it. The final day of the season.

I lifted Nathan's spirits with the news of a much better place to take our stand the next morning. Then we headed back down the mountain. The trip back to the cabin was just as painful as the trip up had been. Muscles were awakened that had been asleep for years. I could almost hear the cartilage in my knees shredding as we pounded down the rocky path. And the gun slung over my shoulder was giving me a stiff neck.

That night we consumed probably an additional pound of saturated fat and a ton of calories. We laughed about killing ourselves with chips, cookies, candy, and hamburgers slathered in mayonnaise. To appease our guilty consciences, we drank diet pop.

We also engaged in another most enjoyable part of a group hunt. Everybody had stories about the events of the day. This guy had a great sighting—three whitetails disappearing into a wooded stand. The next guy saw a huge rack. I should have kept my mouth shut when my turn rolled around. Instead, with full details I shared my discoveries of deer signs. Based on my experience and mostly guessing, I announced where I thought a buck was working and that Nathan and I would like to check out that area when morning light came. I didn't pay attention as the eyebrows went up all around.

After the day we had spent trudging up and down the mountain, sleep came quickly. We were all exhausted as a result of so much fun.

Morning came quickly, too. Our host offered Nathan a ride up the mountain on the four-wheeler, but he refused. A little challenge didn't seem to bother him. Actually, I think his hesitation to ride came from hearing about the wreck the driver had the week before, when he had flipped the machine.

Up on the mountain, we changed into dry clothes again. My heart was racing a little with anticipation as we went to the new stand I had chosen. About ten minutes before daylight we sat down…and the wait began. Around 8:05 A.M. we heard a real reason to get excited.

This noise wasn't chipmunks or squirrels. This sound was different. The leaves had that certain crunch. A buck grunted. In another moment the deer we could not yet see would probably emerge on the flat just below us.

Nathan began to shake with "buck fever." I whispered, "Get ready." We waited as blood rang in my ears.

Suddenly the woods exploded with the blast of a high-powered rifle. Probably a 30-06. Crashing hooves went in all directions. In a moment, everything was silent. And then, in the distance, we heard the telltale snort.

We sat there devastated. Someone had shot "our" deer. Yet we were oddly excited that "something" had happened so close to us.

After five minutes or so, we heard a victory yelp about 150 yards down the hill. Some men do that when they've killed a deer. Someone from another club, or perhaps a local landowner, must have come onto the property. We decided not to interrupt the moment.

We didn't see the others in our party all that day. We had planned our own lunch and told the guys that we would not rendezvous till dark. Since this was the last day of the season, we wanted to take full advantage of every hour. After the big disappointment, we quietly moved to another spot, and I decided to stay with Nathan for the remainder of the hunt. I will never forget the end of that day. Even now it hurts to think about it.

Evening came and the sun began to fall. As the light slowly faded, so did the ability to see very far into the woods. I finally said what had to be said. "Son, it's time to go."

Nathan repeated his response each time I said it. "No! Let's wait. He's comin', Daddy!" At last I said, "Nathan, raise your gun and look down the barrel. Can you see the sights?"

"No, Dad."

"Then don't you think we better go?"

It was a cold, silent trip down that mountain. An occasional moan broke the silence because of the pain in our legs. Both of us were also nursing a pain in our hearts from another year without success. It would be a long drive home with nothing to show for our efforts.

When we neared the cabin we could hear the voices of the two club members. They greeted us with smiles. On the ground next to their car lay a large deer. A nice rack of eight points (a 4 x 4, for you Westerners) graced the animal. It was a beautiful whitetail. I asked, "Who's the proud owner of this trophy?" The answer came from the member who had not invited us on the hunt. "He's mine!" We offered congratulations, and then I inquired, "Where did you find him?" As he answered, my blood ran cold.

Of course there was no way to prove what I suspected, but since that evening I've always wondered if it were true. First of all, we did determine for sure that the gun blast that morning came from his 30-06. Secondly, we learned that the "victory yelp" was part of his tradition.

The fact was, his club dues entitled him to the deer. But the question was, did I direct him to that buck with my conversation the night before? Did he intentionally intercept a first deer that he knew a young hunter could have downed? And did it matter to him if he did? The problem was, it was this guy's third kill that year. I'll never really know the truth, but I'll always wonder.

As I stood there in the glow of the parking lights, my heart ached for Nathan. We helped in lifting the huge buck onto the trunk lid of the man's car, and then quickly packed to leave.

As we offered our farewells, I watched Nathan go over to the deer and, with his tender 13-year-old hand, he stroked the eight points, one by one. Then, as if resolved to wait another year, he put his gear in the back and quietly climbed into our truck.

While we drove away, Nathan's eyes were locked onto that deer. Even when we could no longer see it, he continued to stare out the window. I knew why. He didn't want me to see the tears. I hoped he wouldn't look my way, because I didn't want him to see mine either.

We bounced lightly in our seats as we drove across the huge field to the dirt road that would lead us back to the main road and then home. Before we reached the pavement, I was struck with the reality that my son and I were sharing one of the most incredible moments I would ever spend with a man. We cried together. The tears didn't last long, but the effects of it will last forever. So will the memory.

A nonhunter might be thinking right now, "What's the big deal? Why get all bent out of shape over a deer?" Well, it's much more than that. Nathan had worked so hard, had dreamed even harder, and now had nothing to show for it. For some kids, it's a strike out that causes the last game of the series to be lost, or for others it's a slip on the ice that loses the medal. For my son, that day it was "the one that got away." The same deep disappointment comes for all.

I was grateful to have been there for him when it happened—again. I was able to let him know that the rest of life would not be much different. There would be other disappointments to face, more dreams shattered, and the inevitable feelings of resentment and betrayal that would likely accompany them. From personal experience, I knew the temptation to seek revenge and the desire to give up would crop up again somewhere along the way. However, I told him that when those hard times came, it would be important to confess those feelings to a brother like we had done that day with our tears. I told him that the only way to stop the destructive cycle of ill feelings that often lead to greater trouble was to forgive.

Before we pulled onto the interstate and headed for Nashville, we visited "cholesterol canyon." We found a pizza joint and drowned our sorrow in a deep-dish, thick-crust, greasy pizza. We washed it down with "real Coke." We sat in the booth and discussed everything but deer. (We promised each other to start a diet the next day.)

On the two-hour drive home, Nathan fell asleep. As the miles rolled by, I occasionally looked over at him, and waves of emotions washed across my heart and soul. "He acted like a man today. He showed strength in the face of failure. He's learned so much from this day." I silently thanked the Lord for this friend and for the bond that had grown stronger as a result of going through this small disaster together.

Watching someone you care about go through tough times is never pleasant. As parents, we often want to protect our children and help them avoid the trauma of disappointment. However, there is something valuable in our tough times and losses if we go through them and come out on the other side stronger. That night in the truck I recalled an incident that my wife, Annie, talks about in our book titled *Gifts Your Kids Can't Break*. She says,

> I have found that I need not fear the struggle my kids go through as they grow and learn. It's the struggle that makes them strong enough to survive. Back on the farm in West Virginia, we hatched baby chicks each spring. I'd see those peepers fighting to peck their way out of the shell and my heart would melt. So to help the tiny things, I decided to peel the shell away for them. To my disappointment, each chick I helped in this way soon died. I didn't know they were developing the strength they needed to survive during that struggle to free themselves from the eggshell. When I denied them the struggle, I robbed them of the stamina they needed to live in the outside world. My kindness killed them![3]

I prayed for Nathan that night as he slept that somehow the day's disappointments would yield the fruit of long-suffering in other areas of his life. I also thanked God for the opportunity to learn important lessons like these while deer hunting with my son.

Over the fireplace in Nathan's den, by the way, there now hangs the mounted head of a buck Nathan took the next year on the second day of the season.

6

The Vapor

One thing I like about bow and muzzle loading season is the weather. A slightly cool morning without the need for heavy clothing is a favorite time to hunt. Although the bugs can be a mid-day bother here in Tennessee during the early part of the season, the problem can be solved with proper netting.

I would much rather experience the mid-autumn mild temperatures and endure a few gnats and mosquitoes (but I hate snakes) than sit in bitter-cold weather. However, because my blood type is "doe positive" instead of O-positive, I'll go out and freeze just for the chance of even a sighting. There have been a few mornings that I've been known to look a little like the man in the *Jeremiah Johnson* movie who was found frozen to death with a 50-caliber Hawken clutched to his chest.

For me, hunting from a treestand in extremely cold weather is out of the question for two reasons. One, the wind up there seems to pass right through even the best of clothing. Secondly, if I were to fall, I'm afraid I would break like a china plate on a concrete floor. I would rather snuggle up on the ground against a tree and pursue some degree of comfort, especially for my feet. If my toes hurt, I cannot concentrate. So, my stand is on the ground in the dead of winter, even though the risk of detection is greater.

The times are too numerous to mention when, during one of those bitter-cold days, I've heard that familiar crunch in the leaves or caught a flickering glimpse of a whitetail in the distance. As my heart rate begins to rise to hummingbird levels and the deer approaches, I usually begin that habitual rehearsal of what to do. First, I have to say to myself (if I can remember my name), "Calm down!" and repeat it several times. Then, according to the type of equipment I'm using, I quickly go over in my mind the steps to make the best shot. I then scan the woods for more deer. If there is a lead doe, I wait to see if she is showing any signs that a buck is behind her.

As hard as I try to do everything right, there is one thing that has always frustrated me about being on the ground in frigid weather. It's that annoying choo-choo-like puff of vapor that escapes with every excited breath. I've tried holding it in, but fainting is no fun. I've tried blowing down over my chin toward my chest, but I know I look like a pot of boiling water on a stove. I've tried breathing only through my nose, but the "freezing of the nose hair bringeth pain."

I'm convinced that a deer can spot the movement of fog in the air, and it can alert them to the presence of something unusual. I may be wrong about it, but I still try to avoid "the vapor trail." As hard as I try, I'm never successful.

I can't remember which hunt it was when I first noticed the lesson in the vapor. I'm sure it was not in the midst of a deer sighting, but rather in those hours of waiting when I didn't see anything. It was just me, my cold feet, and the fog I manufactured. I was sort of playing with it, seeing how far out I could blow the vapor. Which direction will the wind take it? (That can be helpful.) What shapes can I make with it? "Hey, that looked like a plate of biscuits and gravy!" (Whoever said sitting on a deer stand is boring?) *But enough playing around,* I thought, *I better get back to hunting. That's why I'm enduring this pain. Right?*

The Vapor

The next breath of vapor somehow caught my attention. Why that particular one? I don't know. But what happened next was special. That vapor of breath hung for a moment, then disappeared. I did it again, and it too went away. The next and the next vanished as well. That's when the Scripture in James 4:14 crossed my freezing brain. "You are just a vapor that appears for a little while and then vanishes away."

I didn't want to think of that! There I was having a wonderful time, then all of a sudden I had to be faced with a "noble thought." Can't this wait till Sunday morning?

It wouldn't go away. That was me out there appearing and disappearing. That was Annie, Nathan, Heidi, my parents, in-laws, brothers, sisters, neighbors, all of us. (It was about then that I could've used a distraction from the impending depression. Something like a ten-point buck would've been nice, but he didn't appear.) I couldn't believe it. Here I was on a deer stand and I was thinking things like, "I'm only here for a little while, a blade of grass in the yard. I'm a leaf headed toward October, an ocean wave that washes up on shore and is never seen again."

Unable to escape the thoughts, I began to seriously consider my own brief life—my "hang time." The realization that my life was like the brief appearance of vapor that quickly disappeared had captured my thoughts. *What will I do with the time I have here? I must make it count for something worthwhile.* In doing so, perhaps a part of me could go on in time. Like the lady who taught a 12-year-old boy how to play the guitar, and her music now echoes through his own melodies. Now he has a son who plays the tunes heard years before when his grandmother used to play. That lady is my own mother. I long, as she did, to do something to ensure that others in the future will know that, even though invisible, I was once visible.

How wisely will we use our time? Have we ever considered what a valuable gift it is? I once heard a challenging scenario that describes time's value. It goes as follows. Suppose I was a banker and I said to you, "If you'll come to my bank each day, I will give you 86,400 dollars to spend any way you wish. The only condition is that at the end of each day you return the portion you do not spend. It will not be added to your account in savings, but instead it will be destroyed. You must promise to spend the money wisely. Do you agree?"

Sure you would! "Mama didn't raise no fool!" you would probably say. I have a feeling you would make every effort to spend the entire amount and as wisely as possible.

The sobering picture is that every one of us goes to the bank of heaven each day and we are given 86,400 seconds of time. When the day is finished, that which we didn't spend or that which we used unwisely is lost forever.

I pray that God would help us, in our hang time, to be a breath of fresh air to our spouses, our kids, family, and neighbors. I pray that He would help us not to waste precious time and to take careful notice of how we act toward those we love. Also, I pray that in our short days His purpose for us in this world will be accomplished.

A momentary encounter with real truths, like the one I was pondering that morning, always yields eternal fruit. I knew I would leave the deer stand that day a different person.

Just how quickly does a man's life seem to pass through time? Perhaps it seems as brief as the time it would take you to read the following lyric:

Seasons of a Man

I am the springtime
When everything seems so fine
Whether rain or sunshine
You will find me playing
Days full of pretending
When a dime is a lot to be spending
A time when life is beginning
I am the springtime.

The Vapor

I am the summer
When days are warm and longer
And the call comes to wander
But I can't go far from home
When the girls become a mystery
And you're barely passing history
And thinking, "Old is when you're 30"
I am the summer.

I am the autumn days
When changes come so many ways
Looking back I stand amazed
That time has gone so quickly
When love is more than feelings
It's fixing bikes and painting ceilings
It's when you feel a cold wind coming
I am the autumn days.

I am the winter
When days are cold and bitter
And the days I can remember
Number more than the days to come.
When you ride instead of walking
When you barely hear the talking
And good-byes are said too often
I am the winter days.
But I'll see spring again in Heaven
And it'll last forever.[4]

7

The Chase

My brother-in-law built the treestand I was in that day on a ridge not too far from "Snooze Point" (named for the afternoon I was caught sleeping there quite soundly). The property was my father-in-law's acreage in West Virginia—a beautiful place in Mason County.

It was about 9 A.M. on a late November morning, and I had not spotted anything even resembling a deer. I was somewhat discouraged and was beginning the mental process of forming plans for the afternoon hunt when suddenly, from the east, I heard a crashing. Oh, how I love that sound! Talk about an adrenaline rush! Just put an IV in my vein when the crashing of deer hooves thunders through the woods, and I can produce a gallon of adrenaline.

Realizing the deer were headed my way, I quickly pulled my rifle to my shoulder and slipped the safety off. I carefully took aim at the buck. He was running right to left on a flat a mere 40 yards away from my stand. With a tremendous blast of the 30-06, I sent a "shaftless arrow" toward him, then number two "torpedo" was delivered. Both deer just kept running. I could tell by the two craters in the ground that I didn't even touch him. I wondered how I could have missed a shot that close.

As they bounded off, I stood there in that treestand totally exasperated. I was also a little perturbed at the buck. I had fired a major high-powered cannon at this guy, and he didn't even look my way. He refused to acknowledge my existence. My valiant attempt went totally unnoticed. I could've been playing a piano in that treestand, and it wouldn't have mattered to him!

But suddenly my mental reverie was interrupted. It was another sound of crashing. Lo and behold, there they came again! It was the same two deer. This time they were running from my left to right. I couldn't believe it. It occurred to me that the old buck might not have known or even cared that I was there but, hey, that doe must have known. I kind of think she was bringing him back by me. "Bless her heart! She's giving me another chance," I said to myself. In fact, I do believe I heard a female voice as they were crashing through the second time screaming, "Shoot him! Shoot him!" (Not really.) I readied, I aimed, I fired. I missed! Two more chances buried in the dirt. Four strikes and I was out. Once again, I had shot the underside of Australia.

Nursing no wounds, that buck ran off into the distance and left me to drown in the sea of disappointment. I tried to settle down, just in case they came blasting through again. I checked my rifle safety, reloaded, and checked to see if I had brought my portable plastic-bottle potty with me. I needed it by then. As I was regrouping and assuming that I wouldn't see another deer for six months, I had a sobering thought.

Though acting on instinct, that buck had cast aside its normal self-protective use of his big ears and keen sense of smell. All that was crucial for his survival in the wild was traded for a chase. A deer's "rut" or mating season lasts four or five weeks of the year, and it is not unusual for the white-tailed buck to act crazy during this period. He may have been acting normally, but in regard to his own safety and his usual overly cautious nature, he was acting like a fool. The bottom line is that, while in "rut," a buck sure makes an easy target of himself.

That's when the word "men" came to my mind. Men can act just as crazy. Just like that buck acted foolishly chasing that doe, men can make themselves just as vulnerable when they cast aside reason and wisdom and chase after something. For us men, it is so easy to set our sights on a desire and forge ahead in hot pursuit, forgetting about everything else that matters. Whether it's a boat and a large-mouth bass, a gun and a grunt call, the fountain of fame, another deal that makes another dollar, or a woman at the workplace, if it causes a man to drop his guard and compromise his values, he is placing himself in a dangerous situation. When pressures or stress or temptation overwhelm a man, it becomes open season on his loyalties to other important responsibilities, and the "enemy" of all that is good will take some shots—sometimes deadly if we're not prepared.

There's nothing anyone can do to stop the white-tailed buck from following nature's call during those four or five weeks of mating season. However, for the male human, there are some definite measures that we can take to help keep our defenses up and protect us from the mistake of throwing away a cautious nature.

First of all, we must understand that the strength to resist and say no to trivial pursuits is found in admitting a weakness. Scripture tells us in 2 Corinthians 12:9 that, "power is perfected in weakness." The cup that is formed by honestly confessing a lack of willpower is the container that will be filled to overflowing with divine strength. A total dependence on God in the face of an overpowering urge to go after a needless thing is His opportunity to confirm His working in your life. So don't be afraid to say, "I am weak but Thou art strong!"

Second, stay away from the forest of fleshly follies. That's where the attractive enticements live. For example, if the pursuit of another woman at your job site is your downfall, make it a point never to be in a room alone with her and never to go to lunch with only her. If you "avoid the very appearance of evil," you will avoid the evil. The solution is extremely simple but terribly difficult to work out.

Finally, keep in mind that, unlike the deer that becomes an idiot only a few weeks each year, man's challenge to maintain his good sense lasts a lifetime, 365 days a year. It is vital to enter each new day with a fresh resolve to fight the unholy urge to chase after the vanities of the flesh. Instead, pray that the pursuit that consumes the desires is one that originates in the Holy Spirit of God who created us. May the phrase from 2 Timothy 2:22 be our chase: "Pursue righteousness."

8

Limitations

I cleared the shooting lanes well in advance of archery season so my human scent would be long gone in my stand area on opening day. I made sure every possible obstruction to the flight of my arrow was removed. I put out my yellow-ribbon distance markers at 15, 20, and 25 yards. That was the extent of my range that year. The lanes were visible in three directions—left, right, and straight ahead. My carefully chosen stand monitored a north/south trail that gave evidence of being well used. Just off that trail to my left stood a couple of white oak trees that were full of acorns, with plenty lying on the ground. The area looked like it would be one of the white-tail's favorite places to visit.

I knew the 14-foot ladder stand was well placed as I climbed into it that morning, so I waited with eager anticipation for the first rays of sunlight. I was so excited that in my imagination I took several deer before daybreak ever came. I was pumped! However, two hours passed without even a squirrel scurrying overhead in the branches and breaking the silence. My excitement slowly waned to sort of bewilderment. As I waited in the quiet of the forest, I began to think about the choice of location I had made for my treestand, and in the process I made an interesting observation as the sun began to warm up the morning.

I looked north, south, and west, and gazed at my distance markers fluttering in the slight breeze. Then, for some reason, perhaps to sigh, I looked straight up into the huge, bright-blue canopy spread above me. That's when it hit me. In the vast expanse of this universe, suspended in one of the myriad galaxies, and tucked away in our immense solar system is a place called Earth. At nearly 8000 miles in diameter and just under 25,000 miles in circumference, there are 57 million square miles of land. How sobering it was to realize that I was limited to a mere 25 yards of shooting range on this planet. (Even if it were a rifle in my hands, 300 yards might be the maximum range—still ever so limited when compared to it all.) Using my short amount of experience—gained in so little amount of all the time that's ever been—I could only hope that this minuscule spot in the universe which I had chosen would be where my skill would meet with opportunity. The animal I was hunting had to come within my incredibly finite boundaries. Otherwise, another hunter might reap the harvest.

Can I be content here? I thought. *Should I move?* If I did, my limitations would only go with me. *Also, what happens if a nice record-book deer comes into view and stands broadside at 40 yards, a mere 15 yards beyond my current ability? What would I do?* You may be thinking, "Quick, get the grunt call and entice him in a little closer!" Let's say I didn't have the call handy. Should I take a shot? Wisdom says, "No!" I'll be smart—I'll wait and hope he moves within range.

It felt strange that morning. I was filled with both a roaring frustration and a quiet peace. I was frustrated because I realized how limited my area truly was, yet my understanding and acceptance of the limitations somehow yielded a restful calm. I didn't have to worry about the territory beyond my "space." I could relax and enjoy the hunting process. Then I began to think of the tremendous benefits of carrying this kind of peace into the rest of life.

One of the best examples of the valuable results of shooting within one's range is found in the life of Pastor L.H. Hardwick in Nashville, Tennessee. He started at the ripe young age of 19 at Christ Church with a handful of people. His distance markers were set very close to his stand. Even when opportunities to move on came his way, he chose to remain faithful and tend the sheep in his fold. Year after year he honed his skills and worked diligently on his gift of shooting straight with the gospel. Today, the size of his range is impressive. Through the years, new converts were added to the faith. The young families had children and eventually grandchildren, and now the congregation is over 3000 strong. Pastor Hardwick, at 65 years old, has seen the fruit of faithfully plowing the field he was given to plow. For 46 years he pressed through rain and shine, lean and fat times, and happy and sad events in the lives of the people. The outcome is pictured in this equation: one man + one pulpit x 45 years = a success that cannot be measured in numbers or in any of man's terms. Only the Hall of Fame in heaven will totally reveal the impact of his life.

I have a feeling that, at times, Pastor Hardwick's contentment to remain with one congregation may have looked like a lack of ambition to other preachers around the country. Nothing could be more inaccurate. Instead, his willingness to work within his limits was a testimony to his fortitude and proved the depth of his vision for the church. Being faithful in the short shots (like maintaining a lasting devotion to his wife, Montelle, and surrounding himself with elders and deacons who made him walk the line) made him a master over the longer shots (like preaching truth to thousands and blessing other parts of the world with missionaries sent out from the congregation).

Great and older men like Pastor Hardwick are an inspiration to younger men like myself. It's easy to fall into the trap of comparing ourselves to the abilities of our peers instead of gaining strength from the time-tested accomplishments of those who have gone ahead of us in this journey of faith. In the field of music that my wife and I are in, there are some tremendously talented people whose success in terms of numbers far exceeds our own. It's tempting to hold our work up and compare it to that of others. However, it only yields discontent. Through the years we have learned to keep our hands to our plow—not theirs.

Annie and I are very much aware that because our lyric content is so specific (family issues), our commercial appeal is limited. We are honestly content with that and do not see it as a weakness. While it is frustrating at times to be difficult to "market," we do not plan to "move our stand." We plan to continue shooting within our range and, in the meantime, work on our ability to effectively use that which is in our hands. We believe those outside our current boundaries will be reached by others in the field. We are responsible only for those that come within earshot of our message. To think that we are the only ones called to reach the world would be as foolish as a farmer who believes that he alone has been chosen to provide crops for everyone on the planet. As we crisscross the country giving concerts, we see ourselves as part of a team of hunters (or in more biblical terms, as "fishers of men"). We are called to be faithful in delivering our "arrows of truth" and to trust God to send them into the hearts of people who need Him.

When—not if—I get "weary in well doing," I find it helpful to get alone and take time to reminisce about a good report, some account of something good that was accomplished. For example, I carry a copy of a letter in my wallet. It is from a young college student who had a friend who was planning to abort her baby. The young lady was unmarried and facing the most difficult decision of her life. The author of the letter wrote to inform us that she had asked her friend to stop by her apartment the following day on her way to the abortion clinic. She had planned to play a song for her troubled friend. The song was entitled "Bring That Child to Me," and it was tucked away on one of our recordings. The lyric is written from a barren woman's point of view and begs anyone contemplating abortion to give the child life and place it in the arms of a couple unable to have children. When the pregnant friend heard the song, she wept bitterly and began to rethink her plans. As a result, she went through with the pregnancy and offered the child up for adoption with the single stipulation that the baby girl retain her name given by her birth mother. The baby's name is Stephanie Anne. Somewhere in the world is a young girl named after Annie and me, and the joy of knowing a life was spared by a simple lyric we wrote helps to keep me faithful in the small things.

Perhaps dark clouds of discouragement have surrounded you and you wonder if your life has been effective at all. Get alone or go for a walk in the woods and look back through time and see if there was someone who came within range of your ability that you may have touched with a love-tipped arrow of kindness or encouragement. I have a feeling you'll be surprised to find how meaningful your days have been. If you do think of someone you have helped, some difficult situation in which you assisted, a kind word spoken to a spouse, a gentle touch given to a child, or a moment taken to help a stranger, be careful to lift the trophies to your Father in heaven. He'll take care of them, treat them like treasures, and store them in the place He has prepared for you.

Today, look around you, set your distance markers, appreciate the hunting ground you're allowed, work on your shooting ability, and trust the Creator of this vast universe to increase your range as time goes on. Happy hunting!

9

Open to Suggestions

Planning a multi-day deer hunt is a process that can occupy the thoughts, conversations, and even the daydreams of anyone who enjoys big-game hunting. Such was the case for my four-day stay at my father-in-law's farm in West Virginia. I made a checklist as long as my arm of all the things I would need from boots to bullets. I checked it twice and didn't miss a detail. I schemed and plotted my course of action. I had "it" bad. By the time the first day rolled around, my expectations for a successful hunt were so high that I nearly ran up the mountain to my stand.

The place I had chosen to hunt was on the remote west end of the property away from houses and humans. My stand was well placed. There were deer signs all around. The weather was great, and I had a 30-06 bolt action that was sighted in and could make three shot patterns the size of a half dollar at 100 yards. I was ready! However, at the end of the third day, I hadn't fired a shot. I didn't understand it. I hadn't seen one single deer.

By the time the fourth and final morning rolled around, I didn't have much hope as I trudged back to the same stand. When 10:30 A.M. came and still no whitetails appeared, I packed up my gear and headed back.

I returned to my in-laws' house for lunch, and Mr. Williamson joined me at the table. He could tell I was frustrated coming back each day without filling my tag, so he offered me some advice. He said, "Steve, if you want to see deer, I suggest you hunt up here behind the house. Quite often I've seen a buck or two come out right at the corner of the fence on top of the hill. Hardly anyone has hunted around the house. I recommend you walk into the woods about 75 paces and set up facing away from the field. Around 4:30, be watching."

Believing that being open to suggestions is a virtue, I decided to abandon my fruitless plans and follow his. At about 4:15 I settled onto a stump near the place Mr. Williamson pointed out. Within 15 minutes I heard a familiar sound—the light crunching of deer hooves pressing into the dry November leaves. Sure enough, there he came. I watched the buck for a few minutes. Finally, his eyes disappeared behind a tree and I slowly raised my rifle. I took aim on his vitals and pulled the trigger.

The buck dropped a few yards from where he was standing when the shot was fired. I took in a deep sigh of relief, for it all seemed to happen so fast, and I needed to gather my thoughts. Then I remembered that a part of the process of harvesting an animal is to record the time of the kill on the game tag. I found my pen, and just as I was writing down the time, it hit me. My watch said 4:35. The shot was made about five minutes before, which put it right at 4:30 P.M. Mr. Williamson's words echoed through my head. I sat there amazed.

"How did he know that my best chance for success would be in this place?" I also wondered, "How did he know for sure the deer would be here this evening?" The answer was simple. For years he had walked every inch of that land until he knew that farm like the back of his hardworking hand. He probably knew when a tree fell on the far side of the property. Why shouldn't he know the habits of the deer that roamed around the farm?

As I stood there looking at the nice-size buck, I was grateful for his advice. Also, I was glad I had chosen to follow it. I shiver to think what I would have missed had I not been willing to listen to him. It was necessary for my success. In fact, any knowledge I possess of hunting is simply a collection of bits of wisdom I have gleaned from other hunters through the years. From conversations in pickup trucks over a thermos of hot coffee to the informative articles in the hundreds of outdoor magazines I've read, I've managed to gather enough know-how to be a successful deer hunter in nearly all of the 30-plus seasons I've ventured out into the woods to enjoy.

Not only in the art of deer hunting is the advice of others a valuable treasure, but even more it is necessary to accept guidance in areas of life beyond the woods. As a father, for instance, I have always needed help. From changing a dirty diaper (field dressing a deer is not half as gross!) to explaining what it means when I say, "This is going to hurt me more than you," I need input from the experts. Fortunately, my best source of instruction was my own dad. He taught me well by being a great dad himself. He had no idea he was teaching a future father some effective techniques when he rubbed the back of my little head while driving down the highway. When he gently placed that same hand on my shoulder as he prayed for me, he was offering another lesson that I still use today as a dad.

Think of all the skills needed in life to succeed. All of us are in need of leadership in our roles as spouses and sportsmen, fiancés and financiers (these sound similar, don't they?), and as friends and family members. In each of these fields, someone who is knowledgeable, whether a professional or a wise friend, is of great value.

For example, what kind of mates would we be without the helpful hints from other men? As a husband, I am always willing to learn. Not all advice, of course, has been useful. One fellow suggested his philosophy on marriage. He said, "I don't try to run her life, and I don't try to run mine!" It seemed to work for him, but I have found a bit of wisdom from another brother to be more beneficial. He said, "In all you do, seek to please your wife first. Be a servant to her, and your marriage will improve daily." His godly advice has stood the test of time and trials. I'm a better husband because of it. My role as a man is not threatened by making a bed or washing the dishes. Instead, I realize that these types of service are actually a testimony to one's manhood. I know this because of the wisdom a friend shared which is found in Matthew 20:26: "Whoever wishes to become great among you shall be your servant." Now that's good advice.

The exchange of wisdom between two people is a blessed event. Good advice, the fruit of experience, tastes sweet to those who hunger for wisdom. Of course, that exchange takes place most often in the times of crisis. A story that best illustrates this is found in a tale you may have heard about the man who was skydiving. He jumped out of the plane, and when he attempted to open his parachute, it didn't operate. As he rapidly fell toward the hard earth below, he scrambled to try to make the thing work. That's when he noticed another fellow coming up quickly from the direction of the ground. As they passed in midair, the skydiver screamed, "Hey! Do you know anything about parachutes?" The other fellow yelled back, "No! Do you know anything about gas stoves?"

The two fellows in that story were more than willing to seek help. To get some advice earlier would have been the best thing to do. Those who are able to cast aside any reservation caused by hindrances like pride or self-consciousness and seek insight from others are to be commended. However, just as Mr. Williamson noticed my silence in the face of a disappointing turn of events and still offered his help, we need to keep our eyes open for those around us who may be facing a difficult time and need some wisdom. Just maybe we can help someone open the chute before it's too late. (As for the guy with the gas-stove problem—I'm open to suggestions!)

10

A Still Small Sound

As a participant in "Archery Camp" held at Maranatha Bible Camp near North Platte, Nebraska, I was privileged to be placed in a large and very comfortable treestand that I called the "Stoner Hilton." It is named after Donn Stoner, who helped build the stand and extended the invitation for my son and me to enjoy a few days in a unique blending of hunting, tournament shooting, and fellowship. The DART System folks were there and provided some realistic scenarios for those who dared to try the big-screen type of target practice. It was a great experience. Plus, I had never seen so much testosterone gathered in one place. All the men were qualified to do the Home Improvement TV show "grunt" when they got out of their cars upon arrival.

The setting at Maranatha Bible Camp is prime deer country. It sits on a winding tributary of the North Platte River, and the surrounding woods are beautiful. The facilities were excellent and the camp staff were first-class from the gate to the supper table. The property we were planning to hunt sits along I-80 in central Nebraska, and the treestand placements made the interstate audible to those who were positioned on the north end of the acreage.

The wind was out of the southeast on that Thursday when we

arrived, blowing about ten miles per hour. The conditions for the evening hunt couldn't have been any better. We were blessed with sunny, beautiful weather. Donn led me to the "Hilton" treestand, and I settled in at 5 P.M. in the cottonwood. The stand was well-placed and it overlooked a logging road that meandered through the woods. A well-used trail crossed underneath. About 5:45, I got a glimpse of a big doe and fawn slowly moving down the road toward me. My adrenaline started to flow, and I was sure my heartbeat was audible. She and the little one disappeared behind a fat Nebraska pine. I knew in about seven to ten seconds they would step into view at about 20 yards from me. I had to make a decision quickly. *Do I finish my weekend hunt, or do I let her go on by and hope for another opportunity with a large rack of horns?* I stood motionless as the huge doe walked out into the small open road. Although I was above her nose, her eyes detected me. Silhouetted against the sky, I was an unusual form. She cautiously went on by, and my bow remained rested in my waist support. I chose to wait.

After a few minutes, my pulse rate returned to normal, and I scanned the woods below me again. The wind picked up a little, and the traffic on the interstate seemed to as well. The combined noises made it difficult to hear one of my favorite sounds in the world. While I love to hear the sweetness of Annie's voice, the children saying "Dad," a congregation singing "It Is Well with My Soul," the lilting brilliance of a hammered dulcimer, the Andy Griffith Show theme song and many other sounds, I would add to that list the distinctive, telltale, slight crunch of the leaves that a deer hoof makes. Somehow, I've developed a keen ability to distinguish it from the scamper of a squirrel or any other noise in the woods.

I was listening hard and realized the competition from the wind and the cars and trucks buzzing by on the interstate was stiff. Yet about 6:15, under the noise of the highway and the wind, I suddenly heard that familiar crunch. It was barely there, but I heard it. Sure enough, I turned my eyes slowly until they would go no further in their sockets. Then I began to turn my head to see if my senses were telling me the truth. Yep! There she was, then another, then two more. They never did come into the opening. To my dismay, I spotted no "hat racks" among the small herd. I spent the rest of the evening observing that group, and eventually the original duo I had seen earlier came wandering by again.

I was tempted to dig for a snack in my pouch that hung on a nail against the tree. Afraid to spook the big guy that may have come through, I stood there as motionless as a statue. Then a thought occurred to me. My mind went back to that moment earlier when I had heard that ever-so-tiny distinguishable sound in the leaves that made me perk up and taste adrenaline again. Not a dozen semis, each with 18 wheels, rolling by 1500 yards away, nor the wind that whipped through the top of the trees was able to hide that sound. Amazing. How did it happen? How could that "ch" sound reach my ears when so many other noises filled the woods?

It was a satisfying thought that I had heard the sound below, and not above, the noise and commotion of the highway and high wind. Somehow that accomplishment excited me as much as the hunt itself. It gave me a confidence that it could happen again because I felt I had gained an ability that is only attainable in time.

However, before my head started to swell too large with pride, a sobering phrase came to me that is found in 1 Kings 19:12 (KJV). The Scripture records the following words: "...a still small voice." The context is a reference to the three great things the Lord's voice was not in when He spoke to Elijah, the prophet: the great wind, a huge earthquake, and a great fire. Elijah responded only to the still small voice.

In the same way I had responded to the small sound of the deer's hoof pressing into the dry leaves that day in such noisy surroundings, so must I give attention to the quiet voice of God. When He speaks, He rarely communicates above the brassy noise of the cares of this life, business concerns, and other distractions. Instead, His voice comes from within, deep in the recesses of a heart that stands quietly before Him. One wise gentleman said, "It's like a bubble that rises to the top and suddenly bursts upon your mind."

Sometimes His voice simply confirms our relationship with Him. Romans 8:16 tells us, "The Spirit Himself bears witness with our spirit that we are children of God."

At other times that voice offers a challenge. When Elijah responded to the still small voice, God then posed a question: "What doest thou here, Elijah?" God didn't need to know the answer. It was Elijah, of course, who needed to know. Like the prophet of long ago, we too need that still small voice to guide us in our modern world filled with so much confusion and distraction.

Perhaps in recent days you have felt a quiet stirring in your heart regarding some important issue in your life. Some questions may keep coming to your mind that, if you answered them honestly, would guide you to a righteous decision. Have you considered the possibility that these inner nudges are not a product of some strength or ability you possess? Instead, they could be God's leading questions.

I remember wrestling one time with a decision regarding whether or not to purchase a certain item. I just couldn't settle the matter until one day some questions came to my mind. *Do I really need it? Do I really have the time it will require to take care of it? And will it benefit in any way my walk with Christ?* I can look back now and see clearly the wisdom in the questions. When I was able to answer them honestly, the struggle ended and I said no to the purchase. I have no doubt that it was the right choice.

It is amazing what we can learn just from the encounter with a deer's steps. I hope the next time you hear the soft crunch of leaves and your heart starts to race that you'll think of another sound that may be heard as well. It just might be that "still small voice."

11

Sunrise

There's something about walking by myself to a deer stand before daylight that makes me a candidate for "chill bumps." Not the little ones that rise up because of a brisk wind that might shoot down the collar. It's the big bumps that jump up because of the fear of what might be hiding behind the next tree. The kind that makes your skin rise up like that of a freshly plucked chicken. I've been in the woods long before dawn enough times to know that the old imagination factory can really process some interesting stuff when the woods are black as coal.

Somehow, a flashlight in the dark is no comfort to me. Whatever is out there will detect my presence even sooner because of the light. So when I can, I enter the woods with my eyes wide open and pupils dilated to the size of dimes.

Remember the character played by Don Knotts in the movie *The Ghost and Mr. Chicken*? That's what I can look like as I walk alone to a stand. There I go, Mr. Macho dressed to kill, yet prepared to pick my heart up off the ground at the first strange sound.

I don't have to be alone when fear grabs ahold. I'll never forget the morning my friend Mark Smith and I headed up a hillside in Tennessee with our bows. I was in the lead, and we were being unusually quiet. It was unbelievably dark. A thick cover of clouds hid a crescent moon, and the woods looked like the inside of a closed casket. Even with Mark a few steps back, I felt jumpy that morning. I stopped to take a breather. Mark took the few extra steps to catch up and then stopped. Suddenly, the silence of the woods was split wide open with an ear-piercing screech. I felt as if I were going to have a coronary on the spot. Straight overhead in the oak tree perched a creature that can take more years off a life than high cholesterol. It was a vicious, two-legged beast that has a most effective device when it comes to stopping a heart. It was what we call a screech owl, and screech it did.

If you've never heard this bird let go a frightening shriek in the middle of the night, then you're in for the scare of your life. It screamed right above me. I screamed too. It was an absolutely horrifying sound, and I felt my flesh crawl on my bones.

My audible response was not repeatable. Actually, I don't really know what I said. You would have to ask Mark. As I stood there consuming a liter of poisonous adrenaline, my friend was thoroughly enjoying life's best medicine: laughter. I think I had tears on my cheeks as I heard the wings of that cursed bird woof off into the darkness. (I've always wanted to ask Mark if I maintained some level of verbal decency in that moment, but to be honest, I'm not sure I want to know. I do know this: He's still laughing about it!)

One nice thing about darkness is that it makes you really appreciate the light. During one hunt in a recent season, I parked at the end of a long meadow on Bear Creek Farm in Tennessee about an hour before daylight. I closed the door to my harbor of safety, hid the ignition keys, and walked up the field alone in the pitch black. All the leaves still clung to the branches on the trees, and the thick canopy made the woods seem even more dense and foreboding. I arrived at my stand about 30 minutes before daybreak and settled in. I was grateful to still be alive and to not have been eaten by the "camo monster." The stars still shone bright overhead, and I knew the morning would present a beautiful skyline. Also, I knew that once daylight came, I could relax, hunt, and not feel hunted.

Slowly the first golden rays of sunlight peeped over the horizon. As I've said before, this is one of my favorite times to be in the woods. As if someone were manually rotating a dimmer light switch, the growing daylight made the shadows give way to distinct shapes of trees and other forest growth. I could see that what looked like the "swamp creature of Cheatham County" in the predawn darkness was thankfully just an ivy-covered oak.

About 30 minutes after the initial show, as though the warm-up act had completed its part, there to the east came the main attraction. Slowly rising above the horizon, so slow in fact that its movement could be noticed only in sections of time, came that huge ball of brilliant fire.

Finally, it was *sunrise*! Just the saying of that word brings comfort from the dark as well as relief and warmth. It's a welcome event. In fact, I've heard that the morning light has caused some who were dying to hold on for another day. There's something about a sunrise that moves our soul. When it happens, it makes me grateful for my sight.

There is a similar dawning that I've come to view as just as enjoyable and incredible. It's those moments when, after wandering around in the darkness of misunderstanding, the lights come on and a truth is revealed. Just as there's relief for this worried hunter when the sun comes up, there's a certain freedom that follows the revelation of truth in other areas of life.

In some cases, the light of understanding that suddenly shines serves to reveal a fact that is valuable but not necessarily earth-shattering. Like discovering that the two tabs on the top of an audio-cassette can be removed to protect a valuable recording. Or finding out that you can put Scotch tape over the place where the tabs once were and record over the contents of a cassette. Do you remember small discoveries like that? Aren't they fun?

However, some revelations are life-altering, even to the point of yielding a freedom that changes one's entire character and personality. The following song lyrics describe an example of a newfound liberty in a life. In this case, the person was bound by unforgiveness until an important revelation transformed his thoughts.

The Key

I cannot tell you how I was hurt but I'll tell you
  I've had some tears
I cannot tell you who it was that turned my trust
  into fears
So I took the pieces of my broken heart
I built some prison walls
And there I've held that offender for years
And this is what I thought,
"He'll never know freedom
As long as I live, I'll never give him freedom."

Then one day the Visitor came to this prison in
  my heart
He said, "You ought to know the truth about the
  one behind the bars.
Yes he's weak and he's weary. He has not smiled
  in years
And you have been successful at keeping his eyes
  filled with tears.
But oh how he longs for his freedom.
These words are the key,
They first came from me,
'Father forgive them'
Come let me show you how to use them."

He said, "Don't you know the offender is rarely
  the one in pain.

> Instead the one who will not forgive is
>   the one who wears the chains!"
> So I opened up the prison door
> I used forgiveness as the key
> And when I let that prisoner go
> I found that it was me
>
> And oh how sweet is the freedom
> It came on the day
> When my heart prayed,
> "Father forgive them,
> Father, forgive them."[5]

How this heart must have danced for joy when the "light" finally came on. Also, don't you know that the ripple effect of forgiveness caused a cleansing that began in that soul and divinely extended to those around him? When a heart is inundated with the powerful light of liberty, that's when the evil and destructive forces that torment a soul will flee like roaches that scatter in a kitchen when the light comes on. Destruction ceases. The light of truth begins to heal. Darkness cannot win over light. The glow of one small candle cannot be snuffed out by all the darkness in the universe.

In many hearts the bitterness, the anger, unforgiveness, and a host of other possible sins have caused the bondage of night to last much too long. The sun needs to rise. A revelation cries to take place. What would it take for the light of truth to begin to peek over the ridge? The only answer to that question is found in what takes place each morning here on the earth.

The next time you're in your deer stand as daybreak arrives, consider this: The sun does not actually rise. The event we have always called "sunrise" is actually a divine illusion. What happens is far more spectacular than we may have realized. Instead of rising, the sun remains stationary. It doesn't revolve around the planet. Instead, it is the earth that makes the move. As it spins on its axis, the earth bows to the sun. What a beautiful picture of the only solution for a human heart that suffers from a void of heavenly light. It must humble itself in the sight of a never-changing God. And at that moment, His light rises up, warms the heart, and blesses all who see it.

God longs to be revealed in every heart, including yours. If you have not allowed Him that divine action, please remember that Jesus said, "I am the light of the world; he who follows Me shall not walk in darkness, but shall have the light of life" (John 8:12). Today is the day of salvation! Let Him into your heart. Then He will gladly say of you, "You are the light of the world" (Matthew 5:14). May the Lord give you courage to allow Him to be the Sonrise in your heart.

12

Blood Bond

I have told my son, Nathan, that if he experiences no remorse after taking a deer, he's simply a killer of animals. If there is remorse, however, he's a hunter. The sad details of inflicting a fatal wound on a deer are not enjoyable to me. However, even in this not-so-pleasant side of a deer hunt there is an important analogy.

First, I must admit that the likelihood of arrowing a deer and not ever finding it is unfortunately a very real possibility. I confess it has happened to me. I once tried for over two days to track a wounded animal and failed. I hated it with all my heart. For that reason we hunters must develop our skill so that our shot placement is most effective. A good hunter is one who is committed to the deer after the shot, especially if the arrow or bullet was off the mark and not in the vitals. Sometimes you never really know until the search begins. It is one of those shoot-and-search episodes that I'll tell about.

When the morning of October 12 came, I was up at 3:30 A.M. and on my way to the farm by 4 A.M. I had looked forward to a day off from office duties and had anticipated staying in the stand all day if necessary (and really wouldn't have minded at all). I made it to the treestand by 5:30, set up my seat, and was ready for action by 5:35 A.M.

I had slightly overdressed (again), and as the breeze picked up, my skin temperature went down because my underclothes were dampened with sweat. It was just after daybreak, and I didn't want to do what I knew I needed to do, but I did it anyway. I put my bow down (only after checking to make sure no critters were watching), dug through my pouch, and retrieved my dry T-shirt. I removed all my upper clothing and stood bare-skinned 18 feet above the ground. The breeze at that height made the word *pneumonia* run through my head, so it didn't take me very long to make the change.

I stuffed the damp clothes in a plastic bag and back in my pouch to minimize the scent. As I scanned the woods, I buttoned up my shirt. I was fiddling with my last sleeve button when the inevitable happened. Behind me, coming down the hill, was a nice-sized doe (our preference for table meat). I froze empty-handed.

I looked behind her to see if she had friends with her, but determined she was alone. Each time she lowered her head to search for acorns, I made a slow, deliberate move to get my compound bow in hand. I also had to get my release out of my pocket, nock an arrow, connect the release, take a heart pill (not really, but it wouldn't have hurt), get the bow up, and turn two slight steps to the left. Somehow I managed to do all these things without her detecting my presence. Because my stand was downhill from the ridge, her path from above me to where she then stood made her eye-level at about 25 yards. I decided it was time.

I slowly lifted the bow and drew back as she stood broadside looking away. My eyes were watering with excitement, and finding her in the peep sight was tough. I pressed the button on the release and the woods exploded. I could not see the flight of my yellow fletching, but I thought I connected because I recognized that familiar run when a deer is wounded. However, I wasn't 100 percent sure.

I looked at my watch, and it was 6:10 A.M. I thought, *My day is over!* Then I realized I was wrong. There was another part of the hunt that was just as important. I waited a necessary 30 minutes and enjoyed the scenery. Then a little before 7 A.M. I dismounted the stand and quietly walked to the spot where the arrow should have been. There was no arrow.

I could see where the deer turned and ran, but the deep leaves made her trail hard to find. I wandered around the area for ten minutes looking for a sure sign of a fatal hit and found nothing. I assumed that if the arrow had made a "pass through," then it was buried in some leaves, so I spent another ten minutes looking for it. Not finding it, I started up the hill a little farther, and that's when I discovered a drop of blood.

It's hard to explain to a nonhunter how the sight of blood affects those of us who stalk into the woods every season to fill a game tag. Each time I'm confronted with two powerful emotions. One comes quickly, and the other settles in later. When I down a deer, the quiet screams of success go off in my mind. I can't classify it as victory because this is not a battle. The deer doesn't shoot back. It's a success because this man has outwitted one of the smartest animals alive. That bright-red color on the ground meant that all the effort of practicing and planning was about to pay off. It also meant I needed to brace myself for the rest of the hunt, take every step carefully, keep my eyes close to the ground, get my plastic fluorescent-pink ribbon out, and leave a trail marker at each place I spotted blood.

Though I headed up the hill slowly, my heart was racing. After the first drop of blood, I found the second about ten yards away, then the third at less distance. At about 40 yards I turned to see the trail of pink ribbons behind me. The line they created indicated the deer was headed up over the ridge and down into the neighboring valley. I topped the hill after two more markers and looked down the other side. The woods were wide open. Which way would I go? I put my face to the ground and didn't look up again until I found one more sighting of blood. When I found it, I knew I had the trail. The deer was bleeding badly at this point, so I stood up and looked behind me. I had covered 75 to 80 yards. It only took one more patch of blood. There ahead of me was venison for the table. Now the messy part of "harvesting" a deer was all that remained. I was back home by 11 A.M.

The second emotion I invariably deal with came that night when I lay down to sleep. In the quiet of a comfortable bedroom and with my head on a soft pillow, I thought through the events of the day. I replayed the scene that occurred that morning, and the distance of time I had come away from the kill allowed me to see the other part of it that I couldn't see due to the concentration involved in the process of shoot-and-search.

When I closed my eyes that night, all I could see was red. That morning the sight of blood felt good. That night the thought of it hurt. That morning the color of success was red. That night a necessary regret clouded the same color. Though it had done nothing to harm me, I took the life of that innocent creature. Once again the pendulum swung from joy to sorrow.

I have often wondered if other hunters go through this same mixture of emotions. I have a feeling they do, but I suppose few ever talk about it. Yet, I believe it is part of the bond that exists between us.

That bond, I have found, is amazingly strong. I see the truth of it often confirmed at the close of a concert. I frequently get the privilege of talking about hunting with folks who have attended the evening, and an immediate friendship often develops. Annie has had to pull me away many times from telling "deer stories" so we can get back to our lodging for some needed rest. I've heard lots of men's wives say, "Oh no! They're talking deer!" The bond is very real, very quick, and always enjoyable.

Then one day it occurred to me that the "fellowship" between hunters is not ultimately based on what equipment we use, where we hunt, how we hunt, or how many "check-in tags" are in our keepsake drawers. Instead, our bond is ultimately based on shed blood. What an incredible picture this is of the fellowship that exists between those who accept and follow the risen Christ. As a result of His crucifixion, we are "blood-bought" brothers and sisters. We were not purchased with corruptible things like gold and silver but with the precious blood of Christ (1 Peter 1:18-19). Our bond is sacred and eternal. It's not based on denomination, building size, or style of worship. That which binds us together is found in these ancient, yet ageless lyrics mentioned in the book of Revelation (5:9):

> You are worthy to take the scroll,
> And to open its seals;
> For You were slain,
> And have redeemed us to God by Your blood
> Out of every tribe and tongue and people and nation (NKJV).

And in a more recent lyric we can gratefully sing:

> There is a fountain filled with blood
> Drawn from Immanuel's veins
> And sinners plunged beneath the flood
> Lose all their guilty stains.

May we all be humbly thankful for the trail of blood that was once found between Pilate's presence and the hill called Calvary.

13

The Appearance

One of the most amazing things about white-tailed deer is the uncanny ability they have to simply appear out of nowhere. With no noise, no hint of their presence, or any warning to help you brace yourself for the shock of turning your head and seeing them just standing there looking at you, they suddenly appear.

In that awesome instant, the heart rate races from 60 to 120 in zero seconds. The eyes quickly enlarge, the jaw sets, and the brain kicks into overdrive trying to figure out how to get your rigid body to respond to its commands. This is one of my favorite parts of going deer hunting.

How many times have you looked at an area of the woods that surrounds you and noticed only the dull, brown leaves and the drab, gray bark of the trees? Yet, upon scanning that same area moments later, you catch a slight movement, and suddenly the flicker of a whitetail causes a shapeless clump of brush to turn into a patch of fur with eyes. Since it is likely the deer had been standing there all along and would not have been detected had you not seen the flicker of a tail, you somehow feel privileged and satisfied to have had a sighting. You may even leave the woods empty-handed, but you don't consider your day a complete loss because at least you had a "close encounter."

It would be difficult to tell you how many times I've been caught totally off guard when a deer mysteriously made an appearance. Many of those times I was involved in various distractions like daydreaming, writing myself a note, eating a candy bar, or waking up from a deep, momentary sleep. A few times, I'm embarrassed to say, I have committed the "bladder blunder." That's the mistake made by moving around in the stand to seek relief only to be surprised by the sound of hooves pounding the dirt as the deer evacuates the area.

Other hunters have told me of additional sightings that were unintentionally mistimed. For example, they were opening the bolt to see if they really did load the gun, they were peeling an apple, taking off a coat, and some were cleaning their glasses when an appearance took place. One of my favorites is this hunter's story:

> The woods were dead silent. The air was hardly moving enough to stir the small wind-detecting thread I had tied to the end of my bow. An occasional buzzing of an insect flying around my head net broke the silence. Otherwise, the woods were so quiet it seemed unreal. I was thinking about what a wonderful day it was to be out of the cage of my office and enjoying such a peaceful setting. How great it was to be refreshed by the sound of silence. I was basking in the soft glow of quiet rest when suddenly it happened—the phone rang. In the cavernous expanse of the big woods, the ring sounded as if it were being broadcast over a sound system constructed for a rock concert. I couldn't believe it. Why on earth I took the silly cellular along I don't know. As I scrambled to turn it off (I wasn't about to answer it), my commotion frightened not one, but two bucks that bolted away behind me. I had no idea they were there. They were out of sight so fast that all I got was a glimpse of

the good-bye wave of two whitetails. I seriously thought about throwing the stupid phone in the creek on my way back to the truck. I would have if I hadn't needed to make a call on the way home!

Sound familiar? I wonder how often the quiet moments of other hunters in the woods are interrupted by things like pagers and watches that beep when it's least appreciated. On and on the possibilities go for some diversion to cost us the harvest of a good memory. In a moment when we least expect it, a deer can appear. If we're not keeping an undistracted watch, we'll have to endure a missed opportunity.

What a vivid picture this is of another appearance that will someday take place. Just as the deer can suddenly materialize in the woods, so will it be that "the Son of Man is coming at an hour you do not expect " (Matthew 24:44 NKJV).

I want to avoid any distraction that would cause me to miss this great event. I don't want to fall short of the goal of being prepared when He does appear. Whether it's a result of taking a spiritual nap, snacking on the foods of the lesser gods, or answering another call to speak for an "overextenders anonymous" meeting, I don't want to be left looking the other way when He comes.

A few things help me stay alert on the deer stand that bear a striking resemblance to the things that can help us watch for the appearance of Christ. One, I try to be rested when I get to my stand. Getting in bed the night before at a reasonable hour is important so that the next morning I'm not nodding off every other minute. It's a precarious feeling to be so tired that I'm tempted to drift off to sleep while sitting on the stand. It's especially treacherous when I'm several feet off the ground in a tree, even though I may be strapped in with a safety belt.

To be rested in the body is good for the soul as well. The physical exhaustion that results from refusing to rest is a display of one's lack of wisdom. Psalm 127:2 warns that "it is vain for you to rise up early, [and] to sit up late" (NKJV). I know from personal experience that getting up at the crack of dawn and working until late into the night is vanity because it destroys longevity. We're like a battery. We're not made with a generator that recharges as we go. We're the type that has to be disconnected from that which we operate, then hooked up to another source and recharged for a period of time. Then we can be reconnected to that which will drain us again of our energy. Being careful to relax on a consistent basis will help keep our minds alert.

Another thing about the issue of rest concerns a lie that I bought into somehow. I was misled to believe that resting could be accomplished through a change of activity. So, to relieve stress, I bought a pair of tennis shoes and started running. In my last year, before my knees gave way, I ran 13 half marathons and one full marathon. Was I resting? *No!* Was I relieving stress? Yes, but I had dropped one type of stress and taken up another.

Some of us believe that a family vacation can be a great stress eliminator. Driving across country with a bunch of kids in a tightly packed station wagon with 800 pounds of luggage to unload each time I stop is not my idea of relaxing. It is suicide.

In my wiser years, I have come to understand that resting is not changing activities. It means stopping, sitting, and generally being a "slug" for a while. How can a battery be charged if it's jumping all around the garage?

The second helpful hint from this harried hunter is that I am conscious of my intake before I go to the stand. I avoid coffee and tea because I don't like what has to happen about an hour into the hunt. Also, I've learned that there are certain foods that trigger other urges that can be a major distraction. I've found it wise to wait until lunchtime to satisfy my appetite.

The parallel this brings to mind in terms of maintaining preparedness on the spiritual stand is how important it is to guard that which we feed the mind. The sources of entertainment, for example, that hinder an alert attitude are numerous. One is visual entertainment.

A man who desires to be a good watchman at the gate of his heart can be quickly lulled asleep by things like TV, cable, rented movies, and magazines. Ask yourself this question: "What do I allow to fill my eyes?" The psalmist David said, "I will set no wicked thing before mine eyes" (Psalm 101:3 KJV). If anyone knew the distraction that straying eyes can cause, it was David. His affair with Bathsheba and all the trouble it caused began with his wayward stares from atop the roof of the palace at a bathing beauty below (read 2 Samuel, chapters 11 and 12).

We must carefully choose what we consume for the spirit. How sad it would be for the Lord to appear while we're off dealing with the effects of unwise intake.

A third tactic I use to help me stay attentive on the deer stand is taking a change of clothes for my upper body. Being able to put on a dry T-shirt after a strenuous and sweaty walk to the stand is a must for the type of outdoorsman I am. I cannot concentrate if my skin is damp and chilly. As much as I don't like switching wardrobes in a treestand, I know I have to do it in order to keep my mind on the hunt.

In the same way, we all face the need to change something in our lives in order to ensure spiritual alertness. Have you ever had a habit, for example, that you knew was a hindrance to a healthy body and mind? Because of this addiction you knew your temple was not a clean place for the Spirit of God to dwell. At some point, however, you decided to change, and by the grace of God and His strength to help you with self-discipline, you became a different person. As a result, your senses are more keen. That's the kind of change I speak of that will help us be ready for the appearance of Christ.

Please keep in mind that Christ will return someday to earth. We can be ready when "in the twinkling of an eye" the Savior appears.

We don't have to be caught unaware. May we not faint, but be faithful to stand guard until that blessed moment. And instead of taking home a trophy, we will be the ones who are carried home by the divine Hunter who will appear and find us watching and waiting for Him!

14

Lost and Found

During a hunt with several other archers, an incident occurred with Nathan that he has given me permission to tell. This episode does no damage to his reputation, but does provide a very good lesson that can be learned only in the wild.

The schedule at the camp was as follows: 5 A.M.—wake up and get ready for breakfast; 6:30—head to the stands; 10:30—return to camp; 12:00—lunch and range shooting; 3:00 P.M.—head back to the stands, return to camp at dark for an evening meal, more range shooting, and tournament competition.

It was after the 10:30 A.M. return to camp that Nathan and I took a walk. He carried a video camera, and I packed my bow and broadheads. Around 11:15 A.M., as we were quietly slipping through the woods, I informed Nathan that it was time to head back and grab some lunch. Before we returned, I asked him to drop off the main trail we were on and head into the woods about 200 yards south, go east 100 yards, and then turn back north and return to me. Though we both knew it was not highly effective for archery, he agreed to this short "drive," and I took a stand along the edge of the woods and waited. I had instructed Nathan to move very slowly, so the deer, if there were any, would hopefully not be running if I saw them.

I waited 20 minutes, then 25 minutes passed. After about a half hour I began to wonder, "Is he moving that slowly?" At 45 minutes I decided he must have come out at the wrong place, missed me, then went on back to camp. So I returned to the lunch hall and discovered that he was not there and no one had seen him. I went ahead and tried to eat lunch, hoping he would walk in while I was there. I may have eaten a bite or two, but I don't remember because I was checking for my son every time I heard the door open. After an hour of anxiously waiting for him, I was becoming seriously concerned.

I borrowed the camp pickup and drove to the area where I had left him. I got out and called his name as loudly as I could, but there was no response. I drove to another part of the property and still found no sign of him. A knot of fear was tightening inside as I headed back to camp hoping he had shown up. He was not there.

A gentleman and new friend at the camp, Ken Malott, recognized my growing despair. He was perceptive enough to note my anxiety and offered his assistance. We took off on a search.

By then two and a half hours had gone by, and I was beginning to imagine some unpleasant scenarios. I thought, *He's fallen and broken a leg and can't get up. He's definitely lost. He's probably been eaten by either a mountain lion or one of those guys from the movie* Deliverance.

As we scanned a field along the entrance road, we saw a car approaching in the distance. It was heading into the camp and coming our way. Ken suggested that we slow down and see if by chance Nathan was in that car. Lo and behold, he was! What a relief it was to see his face again.

The two vehicles stopped side by side in the road, and a happy reunion took place. We sincerely thanked the fellow who had taken the risk to pick up someone who looked as ragged as Nathan. The four hours of beating through the bushes had left him drenched in sweat, minus some articles of clothing, and hungry and thirsty enough to devour a mule down to the hoof. Grateful to be reunited, we drove back to camp.

Nathan told us that when he dropped into the thick woods, he walked far enough from the sound of the interstate that he could no longer use it as a reference point for direction. He turned in a direction he thought was north, but didn't realize he had actually made an easterly turn. Instead of heading toward it, he was walking parallel to the highway. He became disoriented, and without knowing it, he turned south. The sun was straight overhead, so it was hard to tell which way was east or west.

About an hour into his "adventure," Nathan thought to turn the video camera on. His commentary into the microphone of the camera, which we listened to later, was rather interesting despite his ordeal. He taped things like, "I can hear it now on 'Current Affair,': 'Boy gets lost and his fate is captured on the very camera he was carrying. Stay tuned for this tragic story.'" As he pressed through the heavy brush, a strain in his voice could be detected when he said simply and sincerely, "Sorry, Dad!" He also sang a lyric to a song he had recorded on a CD that says, "Sometimes it seems that I just keep on circling, never getting closer to my home…" It's video footage that would move the heart of any parent.

With Nathan back and safe, I headed to my treestand that evening again to hunt. After settling in, I began to think about my son's experience that day. First, I was truly thankful that he was found. The anxious moments fortunately were just that—only moments. I've heard of some parents whose children get lost and are never found. In the flat midwestern state where we were hunting, it would be tough to get entirely lost for days like you could, for example, in Colorado. If you walked a straight line, eventually you would come to a road you could follow. You might end up in a small town or come out behind a truck stop, but sooner or later you would find civilization. But Nathan didn't know that. As far as he was concerned, his wilderness experience was as real as though he were lost in the remote regions of the Colorado Rocky Mountains. The frustration and fear he had to fight were just as significant.

It could not be minimized, especially in the heart of such a young man.

Second, something occurred to me as I tried to imagine myself in his place. When I sent him off and we disappeared out of each other's sight, our priority was deer. All that occupied our minds was the anticipation of seeing "fur" and the possibility of hearing the twang of the bowstring as an arrow was launched at a trophy. However, in that moment when Nathan (and I) realized he was lost, our priorities took a 180-degree turn. Nathan's thoughts turned to being found. Mine turned to finding. His thoughts were on survival—food and water. I had no appetite. His thoughts were, "What will I tell Dad?" Mine were, "What will I tell Annie?" But nowhere in our minds could you have found the words "white-tailed deer."

I continued to think about the day's lessons as the sun slowly sank behind the western horizon. Nathan had related to me that his first thought, once he knew he was lost, was to pray. That made his dad proud! It occurred to me that the spiritual picture that could be drawn from his statement was very clear. It's only when a person realizes that his or her soul is lost that there will be a cry for help. I love the Christian phrase "get saved." That is exactly what happens. A person wanders around in a wilderness of some kind (self, drugs, sex, hobbies, occupation, etc.). Then, through the work of the Holy Spirit, a realization of "lostness" hits and the priorities quickly change. All that seemed important before fades in the light of the need to be rescued.

Another thought I had that evening was of parents who have watched a child disappear into the thick woods of the world, and who are now desperately praying their wayward son or daughter will be found. I confess that I was one of those kids. I wandered off into the jungle of enticements offered by this world. Thankfully, my dad and mom came looking for me in their vehicle of prayer. One day, at the age of 24, I realized I was lost and had no idea where I was spiritually. It was then that things like music, fame, and appearance took last place in order of importance. That revelation in my heart, I believe, was a product of the prayers of a righteous man and woman who daily begged God to rescue their son. For those of you parents who long for God to bring your child home, perhaps the following lyric, entitled "Reachable," written in the countryside of Tennessee, might be helpful.

Reachable

There's a boy in his mother's prayers
'Cause lately she's been aware
That he's been drifting
Too far from the shore.
And she's beginning to believe
The boy is getting out of reach
Weary Mother, don't you worry anymore.

'Cause the boy is reachable
I know he's reachable
And to God he's visible
And all things are possible.
'Cause if the Lord can reach His hand of love
        through time
And touch a cold sinner's heart like mine
The boy is reachable, I know he's reachable.

And there's a girl on her Daddy's heart
'Cause lately they've drifted apart
And the company she's keeping
Leads her further away.
And he's beginning to believe
The girl is getting out of reach
Oh, weary Father, hold on
Heaven hears you when you pray.

And the girl is reachable
I know she's reachable

And to God she's visible
And all things are possible.
'Cause if the Lord can reach His hand of love
    through time
And touch a cold sinner's heart like mine
The girl is reachable, I know she's reachable
If this boy is reachable, anyone is reachable.[6]

The moment Nathan realized he was lost and began his pursuit of his dad is a picture of repentance. It's the turning away from earthly priorities, and going in another direction toward a heavenly one. I, as Nathan's father, in that same hour was longing for the lost one. That's love. Nathan told us that when he broke through the woods and found a road, he decided to follow it, hoping it would lead him to some help. The road he found is a picture of Jesus, the only Way to our Father in heaven. Our reunion on the road that day is symbolic of salvation. You might be reading these words and at this moment realize your soul is lost. Whoever you are, embrace the awareness. That's the Holy Spirit speaking to your heart. Turn away from priorities rooted in this world. That's repentance. Follow the road of Christ. He is the Way. You can come home to the heavenly Father. That's the good news.

"For God so loved the world that He gave His only begotten Son, that whoever believes in Him should not perish but have everlasting life" (John 3:16 NKJV).

15

Things Aren't Always As They Seem

The alarm went off at 3:45. Because I was going to be spending a day in the woods, I had no problem getting out of bed. On the mornings of a planned hunt, you would think there was a catapult built into my mattress which is triggered by the alarm clock. Of course, on days when our concert schedule calls for an early-morning departure, getting up can prove to be quite painful. It's not that I don't like my work. I just don't find it enjoyable to risk my life once again on an airplane that was probably built by the lowest bidder. (Flying is no fun for me. I agree with the fellow who said, "I wish they wouldn't call airports 'terminals'!") Also, I don't care to drive in rental cars on strange highways where people are talking on the phone, doing their hair, and going through file cabinets. Furthermore, I'm not crazy about laying my head on another hotel room pillow that I know has been drooled on by dozens or maybe hundreds of other people. I prefer my own drool, thank you! But this was a morning I was going to get a break from that routine by being "in the wild," so waking up was no problem. By 4:10 I was willingly on my way to Hickman County, Tennessee, and at 5:30 A.M. I was comfortably perched in my portable treetop easy chair and enjoying my early start at engaging in the "think time" I mentioned in the introduction to this book.

As I sat there in the brisk morning air searching my mind for interesting memories, I had to be careful not to do what I used to see my Grandpa Steele do while he sat on the front porch of his house. I can still picture him sitting for a long while and not uttering a sound. Then suddenly, he would start to laugh out loud. Whenever I was there, I would ask, "What are ya thinking about, Grandpa?" I always enjoyed his answer because there would be some humorous story in his thoughts.

The same thing has happened to me in the quietness of a deer stand. I have recalled some events in my life that have generated a chuckle or two. In the woods, I have to control myself, however, lest by laughing out loud I give away my presence and scare away the deer.

That morning I had one of those fond recollections. It involved my Grandma Chapman. I remembered she was sitting on the back porch of the "big house" where she raised her 11 kids. All of them had moved away—about 100 yards. My dad and mom lived even closer than that in a nearby small frame house until I was ten years of age.

It was a summer day in my seventh year. Grandma was snapping the green beans she held in her apron and dropping them in a pan on the floor next to her chair. My mother decided it would be a good day to complete the job of cleaning the eaves of the house. With a broom and a kitchen chair in her hands, she headed out the front door. In tow were my sister and I. We had been given brown paper bags to use for gathering the cobwebs and old birds' nests Mom would knock to the ground with the broom.

She climbed onto the chair and proceeded to gouge the broom into the eaves on the backside of that little white house. Suddenly, Mom got the surprise of her life when she stuck the broom into a hornet's nest. The angry hornets came swarming toward us, making an ominous sound. It was a frightening sight as well. They looked like "quarter pounders" with massive wings. We all screamed and threw our arms about and danced around, trying to avoid the hornets' revenge.

I don't know how I thought of it, but as fast as my little six-year-old legs could carry me, I ran toward the dirt road near our house. I knew it would lead to Grandpa Chapman's store, where I would find safety. When I took off, one lone hornet decided I was going to be the object of his retaliation. Someone was going to pay for destroying its home. I could hear it angrily buzzing behind me. I screamed at the top of my lungs and pumped my legs like an Olympian running the 100-yard dash.

Right at my heels, I was thankful to discover, was my mom. Realizing her son was under attack, she decided to rescue me by killing the hornet with the broom.

As I dashed down the little dirt road toward the store, my mom swatted repeatedly at the hornet while running close behind. By this time, we were in full view of Grandma. She heard me screaming as I ran, and she saw my mother wildly swinging the broom behind me. However, she couldn't see the hornet. I always get a chuckle out of imagining what she must have thought. I'm sure it was the worst. In fact, the next green bean she snapped was probably, in her imagination, my mother's neck!

I made it to the store and, up to that point, I was an "unstung hero." Unfortunately, the porch was too high for me to jump onto quickly. When I slowed down to do it, that's when I felt the hornet bury its fiery stinger into the back of my leg. It felt like a baseball bat had knocked me to the concrete. I went sliding across the porch gathering "road rash" on my little belly. I remember crying in pain as I lay on the porch of the supermarket.

About that time, my grandma appeared on the other end of the storefront. She marched over to my mom and promptly gave her a good talking to about what she had just seen a few moments earlier. Oh, how I wish now that I would have had the wisdom and the composure to quickly stand up, brush my little self off, dry my tears, and say, *"Grandma, things aren't always as they seem!"* However, she eventually realized the truth of what had happened and all was well (except for the throbbing pain in the back of my little leg).

After all these years, I still shiver when I remember my bout with that hornet. But that morning on the deer stand, I enjoyed a controlled chuckle once again when I thought of my grandmother's perspective of my predicament. Though it was traumatic, the years of time that have passed have helped me glean some valuable insights from the story.

As hard as I ran from that angry hornet, it still caught me and inflicted its pain in my life. I wish I could've outrun it, but I suppose there was something to learn from it. Perhaps I needed to realize that in the course of time there would be other painful experiences that would overtake me. And while going through them, I would need someone to battle on my behalf and be there to comfort me if hard times knocked me down. As it turned out, it was only two years later that I found myself once again in a terrifying situation.

At the age of eight, I became quite sick and developed a swelling in my throat that was accompanied by a loss of weight and a darkness under my eyes. Alarmed at the symptoms, my parents took me to see the doctor. They held me tightly as he examined me and then announced that an operation would be necessary. I spent three fear-filled days in the hospital as they did a number of tests on the tissue they had removed from the lymph nodes in my neck. The frightening buzz of the word *cancer* gripped my parents. They saw me running scared.

Just as my mother tried to kill the hornet that day with the broom, I know my parents were flailing the weapon of prayer at the attacker that was trying to harm their son. Yet, for some reason—still unknown—the "hornet" did its dastardly deed. What then? All that remained for them was to stay close and offer comfort and help. And that they did by placing me into God's hands as well as the care of a compassionate and knowledgeable doctor.

We were all relieved to hear that the entire tumor had been removed and that my life would go on. The doctor said that had we waited a few more weeks, the outcome would have been far different.

Going back to the hornet horror, Grandma was puzzled by the scene in the distance as I ran screaming down the road ahead of my mother. In the same way, others will stand by in bewilderment and watch as loved ones go through tough times. Tragedies like divorce, illness, and injury, or the loss of a job or self-respect will leave us all with questions. Yet, there'll come a moment when, like Grandma Chapman learned the truth about the bee and me, sometimes we will never know the reason for the "sting" in the lives of loved ones. It's important for them to know when the hard times come, they're not alone. We need to be there for them when they buckle under the pain.

As I enjoyed my recollection of my grandmother that morning on the deer stand, I began to really miss her, as well as all my grandparents. The joy of their memory often intensifies the sadness of their absence. I miss my Grandma Steele. I long to sit beside her again in the porch swing. I miss hearing my Grandpa Chapman say to us, "Put your feet out and be a good horse!" I miss Grandpa Steele's funny stories. And I miss those three special heartwarming words my Grandma Chapman would always say to me when I went to her house: "Want a sandwich?"

I often grieve over their absence. Yet, I know I can do so with hope. I believe we all will see our departed loved ones whose lives belonged to Christ. I have an assurance that the painful grief in the hearts of the living who are left behind by those who pass on, will be eliminated on that glorious day that is described in 1 Thessalonians 4:16-17 (KJV):

> For the Lord himself shall descend from heaven with a shout, with the voice of the archangel, and with the trump of God: and the dead in Christ shall rise first.

> Then we which are alive and remain shall be caught up
> together with them in the clouds, to meet the Lord in
> the air: and so shall we ever be with the Lord.

I look forward to that day! I have a feeling that many of you do as well. And until that wonderful day arrives, may we be found faithful in the race against all that would knock us down. And if someone has been knocked down by the hardships of life, let's give him a hand and help him up.

I wondered that day in the treestand what I might have been able to see if my spiritual eyes were opened. Could I look into the heavens and see the great cloud of witnesses mentioned in Hebrews 12:1? I felt that were I allowed to do so, I would see my Grandma Chapman leaning over the balcony of heaven, saying, "Steve, hold on. Don't give up. Be faithful to finish the race. 'Lay aside every weight that would easily ensnare you.' What you see with your eyes may sometimes look bleak but, remember, I have a different view of things. Things aren't as they seem. God is in control!"

Thank God for deer stands and think time!

16

God Will Repay

Nathan and I hoisted our rifle slings over our shoulders and quietly walked away from the truck and into the predawn darkness. We were excited but managed to keep our conversation at a whisper level as we stepped side-by-side toward a huge, harvested cornfield we had to cross to get to our deer stands.

With the temperature around 35 degrees, a clear sky, and hardly any wind, the weather was perfect for chasing whitetails. But there was something about the morning that made it even more joyful for me. I was hunting with my son again. Because of our busy schedules, it had been far too long since our last outing.

When we reached the edge of the massive field, our talking ceased as we began the challenge of crossing it, moving through the harvested rows without making a lot of noise. While we concentrated on carefully stepping over and around the nearly shin-high stubs of cut stalks, I was also busy pushing back a thought that wasn't welcome. I had a feeling that the hunt my son and I were sharing this morning might be the only one of the season. In an effort to savor every moment, I whispered, "Nate, let's stop here and rest a second."

Nathan halted.

As if we both were thinking the same thing at the same moment, we turned around to look at the sky toward the east. I stated the obvious. "Looks like we got here a little later than we should have. Sunrise might beat us to our stands."

Nathan adjusted his rifle sling. "I've been longing for quite a while to sit in a deer stand and watch that old sun come up again. Thanks for coming with me, Dad."

"You bet, Buddy. And before we hurry on across this field, there's something I forgot to tell you about this hunt. I know you'd like to put some venison in your freezer—and I hope that happens. But if we take two deer this morning, I know a family that could sure use one. They're going through hard times right now, and a juicy doe would be a blessing for them. So I'll be pulling the trigger too if I get a chance."

Nathan looked back toward the east again, and I could tell he was contemplating my idea.

"Well, Dad, if I get one and you don't, it'll go to that family. Sounds like they need the meat a lot more than I do."

I wondered if the low light allowed him to see the look of love and satisfaction on my face. "Nate, that's mighty kind of you. Are you sure about that?"

"I am. I'm happy to do it."

By the time we finished our brief exchange, the light was up enough that the line of trees on the far side of the field was discernible.

"Now we're in a little bit of hurry, Nate. It's gonna be tough to keep our walking quiet in this corn debris. But we'd better put it into the next gear if we're going to get to our stands at a decent time."

We still had quite a ways to go before we would split up at the field edge and go to our stands. We would have preferred to complete the crossing in the dark, but it was as though someone had flipped a switch on. The entire farm seemed to suddenly light up around us. The cloudless sky had allowed the sunrise to happen earlier than we'd expected, and within a couple of minutes we had legal shooting light.

We were still about 300 yards from the edge of the field where we would go our separate ways. Between us and that point was a feature of the terrain I knew was a favorite pass-through spot for the local whitetails. It was a sizable depression about 100 yards wide that spanned the width of the field. For some reason, the deer seemed to use it a lot as a crossing, perhaps because the wall-like grade on both sides helped them feel protected.

I stopped for a moment and whispered a reminder to Nathan about what was just ahead. "We'll want to be especially careful as we get to where we can see down into the depression in this field. There might be some four-legged critters in it. If there are, in this light you might be able to get off a shot if they don't spot us first."

Just as we took a step, Nathan grabbed my arm.

"Dad! I think I just saw the tops of some ears. Something flickered at the ground line about 50 yards from here, where the field starts to drop into that low area!"

I immediately lay flat in the field. Nathan followed suit.

"Let's wait here a minute," I whispered. "Might be something walking out of that depression."

Nathan put both of his elbows on the ground and got his .270 into firing position. I dug for my binoculars and scanned the area ahead. We both saw the form of a deer coming out of the low area. It was walking right toward us! When I heard the soft click of Nathan's rifle safety being turned off, I stayed motionless. I knew he was sighting the deer with his scope.

Stepping straight in our direction, the deer suddenly stopped and stared our way. We weren't sure if she had spotted us, but we knew our forms must look out of place to her. We hoped we appeared unhuman. And we hoped that what little wind was blowing wasn't moving from us to her.

Nathan's voice held the excitement I'd hoped to hear this day. "I've got her in the scope, Dad! But unless she turns broadside, I don't have a shot."

"I've got her in the glasses. She's a nice one."

As deer usually do when something unfamiliar shows up in their world, the doe showed signs of unease. Unfortunately for her, the anxious feelings prompted her to take a couple of sideway steps while she pondered whether or not to run. Her hesitation was costly.

The blast of Nathan's rifle broke the silence of the calm morning. The doe kicked high and ran back in the direction she'd come. She disappeared into the depression.

Nathan and I quickly got up on our knees as he chambered another shell.

"You hit her good, Nate! She won't go far."

Nathan clicked his safety to the on position and threw his left arm around my shoulder. "Well, that was quick. But I'll take a moment like that any day of the year! *Whew!* That was exciting."

I returned the one-arm hug as we looked in the direction the doe ran. We were sure she'd expired just out of sight. We stood and walked toward the crest of the depression. When we got about 25 yards from where we would be able to see into it, Nathan grabbed my arm.

"Dad, there's a deer!"

"Where?"

"Going up the other side of this low area! Maybe I didn't hit her as well as we thought."

"Maybe not," I answered as I dropped to my knees.

Nathan quickly sat down in the field and put his elbows on his knees, getting ready to fire another round. He scoped the escaping deer and clicked the safety off. "Guess I'd better close the deal on this doe. Fire in the hole!" he whispered.

The concussion of the shot seemed to shake the ground as we watched the doe collapse right where she was standing. We kept our eye on her for 30 seconds or so. Feeling very sure she was finally ready to tag, we enjoyed another celebration. We got up and walked toward the heap of venison that awaited our care. When we reached the point in the field where we could see into the entire depression, we stopped in our tracks. We didn't immediately understand what we were looking at. There was a second deceased doe lying right below us.

We didn't say a word to each other for a few moments. I finally verbalized the reality of what had happened. "Nate, that doe below us is the first deer you took a shot at. The second one on the other side must have been behind her and was leaving the area when you spotted her. You just got yourself a double! Now ain't that a deal."

Nathan didn't smile like I thought he would. Instead, his expression turned worried.

"Wow! The Lord knows I thought I was finishing that first doe off when I took the second shot. But what about the law? Am I in trouble, Dad?"

He seemed deeply relieved when I answered, "Two things, Nate. Both deer were taken with an honest heart. I don't think we'll have any problem putting tags on these does. And you just blessed your family and another family with a lot of good eatin'. And you had a ton of excitement doing it! It doesn't get any better than that!"

We tended to the "pleasurable" task of field dressing the pair of does. Because Nathan has a unique allergy to the dander of deer, I did most of the work—but we both did our share of talking. Most of it was about how so much action was packed into such few minutes. We also dwelled on how totally surprised we were to discover that the two shots had yielded two filled tags. We knew this was a morning we would never forget.

As it turned out, the short-but-sweet hunt was our only outing that year. But we enjoy recalling that unforgettable morning! Just to name a few of the great memories I attach to that day...

I recall the early ride together in the dark, sharing the familiar feeling of anticipation while driving to the spot, loading our rifles at the truck, and then walking into the blackness of the morning.

And the smell of expended gun powder hanging in the still air after Nathan took his first shot lingers in my mind.

But there is one other memory of that morning that is especially meaningful. It was the offer Nate made to give away his deer if he got one, especially knowing it might be his only chance to hunt that season. Proverbs 19:17 sums up what happened that day. "He who is gracious to a poor man lends to the LORD, and He will repay him for his good deed."

I am convinced that God, whose ear is not deaf to our hearts or words, heard Nathan's response to the news of the needy family and had taken into account his intended generosity even before we saw the first deer. The "lending to the Lord" had already happened in Nathan's heart. The second deer was the repayment for the good deed that had been promised.

What an incredible thrill to see firsthand how God keeps His Word when it comes to blessing those who bless others. It is an indescribable joy for me to see God demonstrate such an awesome truth while on a deer hunt with *my* only begotten son in whom I am well pleased.

17

Scars of Love

While my nerves settled back to a level that didn't cause my hands to tremble so much, I pressed the number "1" on my flip phone and held it down. As I waited for the ring tone to sound in my ear, I mentally replayed the shot I'd just taken at a huge buck. My thoughts were interrupted when after only two rings my wife, Annie, answered. Following our hellos, I immediately told her what had happened only moments before.

"Babe, I was sitting here in the ladder stand overlooking a field, and everything unfolded in an instant! I was reaching around to my left to get an apple out of my pack that was hanging on the tree—and that's when I saw him! He came walking along the edge of the woods, headed right by me. I hardly had time to pull up the bow and take aim. I had to shoot him as he walked 'cause I got so excited I forgot to try to stop him with a mouth grunt. He took off across the field after the arrow found him."

"Do you think you got him good?" Annie asked.

"I do! I saw the arrow enter just the right spot. Double-lunged him, I'm sure. I don't think he'll go far. I'm not sure how many points he has, but he's got to be at least an eight. I'm guessing he weighs 160 pounds or so. For this territory, that's well above average.

He wasn't but 10 or 12 yards from me. He was close enough that in the few seconds I had to look at him I noticed a nasty scar on the side of his head. It was probably from all the fighting he's had to do for the women in his life!"

Annie chuckled and then responded, "Well, from what you've told me about the warfare that bucks engage in for the cause of *love*, it's no surprise to me that he'd be wearing the signs of it!"

I smiled at the emphasis Annie gave to the word "love." "Yep," I responded. "It seems that the old boy paid a price for his affection for the girls. I'm sure glad we human bucks don't have to engage in such conduct—although I would if I had to when it comes to you."

Annie laughed again and added, "Well, aren't you a sweet talker. I appreciate your willingness to do battle for me, but you'll be glad to know it won't be necessary. I'm your doe, and this doe says congratulations on the outcome of your morning. Sounds like you're going to be occupied for a while longer. I'll look forward to seeing you and the battered beast when you get here. Call before you leave the farm, and I'll have a late breakfast for you when you get home."

I closed the cell phone and put my head back against the tree to rest from all the excitement. As I paused I thought, *I really would bleed for that woman if I had to. She's definitely worth fighting for!*

A few years have passed since that unforgettable hunt, and I still enjoy the memory of my conversation with Annie after that hunt. I also love recalling the thrill in her eyes when I got home. She looked into the bed of my pickup at what turned out to be a big-bodied ten-point with at least five scoreable short stickers...six if I lived in a state that follows the "if you can hang a finger ring on it" rule.

Because most deer hunters deeply value their memories, the details of a hunt like I had that day come back to us at the oddest of times. In places like airport gates where we might have some extra time to think while waiting on a flight to board, or while we're driving solo through the country and alone with our thoughts. And for some, it can even happen in the church pew when our minds drift during a sermon we should be listening to instead! I admit I've engaged in many replays of hunts in all the places I just mentioned. But more recently, the memory of a specific thing about the ten-point came to mind in a setting I didn't expect. I was working on a song lyric that eventually was titled "Scars of Love." When you read it, you'll understand the connection:

Scars of Love

On the faces of the soldiers who have fought
    for our freedom
On the arms of the brave ones who have saved
    us from the fires
On the knees of the mothers who have prayed
    for wayward children
You will find them...

Scars of love on the skin
Proof on the outside of what lies within
Let us all bow our heads
And thank our God above for all the scars,
Scars of love

On the shoulders of the farmers who have
    carried our hunger
On the backs of the miners who have warmed
    us with their coal
On the lips of the preachers who have never
    feared the truth
You will find them...

Scars of love on the skin
Proof on the outside of what lies within
Let us all bow our heads
And thank our God above for all the scars,
Scars of love

And on the hands and the feet
Of the Carpenter from Galilee
Can you see...

Scars of love on the skin
Proof on the outside of what lies within
Let us all bow our heads
And thank our God above for all the scars,
Scars of love[7]

Just like the mature ten-point I'd taken was wearing the signs of his willingness to battle for something he considered worth fighting for, there are countless humans who have done the same. I listed only a few in the limited space of the song lyric, but I have no doubt you could add many more.

I venture to say that on the skin of most of us who have lived long enough someone could find outward evidence of the love we have inside us for others. Some scars might be the results of accidents while doing something with or for people. Still they are there as signs of deep affection. Other scars are the products of deliberate acts of love. I bear on my own face the product of an opportunity I had several years ago to explain to one of my children about both types of scars.

The church my family attended was planning a scramble golf tournament, so I was getting in some practice in the front yard with one of my irons. As I was making sure my fabulous swing was still not there, my daughter, Heidi, who was about eight years old at the time, came out of the house and saw what I was doing.

"Dad, can I try that?" she asked.

"Sure, Sweetheart!"

I handed her my five iron.

Heidi choked up on the shaft, stepped back, and took a full swing. I was pleasantly surprised when I saw how natural she seemed in moving the club. At that moment the word "scholarships" came to mind.

"Heidi, you have a very fluid swing. Let me show you a couple of things I've learned about handling a golf club."

I backed her up to me and, standing right behind her, I said, "Widen your stance a little, tilt your head down and keep it in place, and keep your shoulders level. Now swing the club back and forth over that white clover in the grass."

When Heidi heard the word "swing," she translated it as just that. She proceeded to take a full swing. Apparently at the last millisecond she realized what would happen because I was so close behind her so she tried to stop the club. Because the club was a little heavy for a youngster, she didn't quite get it done. It whipped in her hands and caught me square on the cheekbone with the front edge of the blade.

I reeled off into the yard holding my fingers over the spot on my face where the hard metal had hit. I could feel a knot growing. I looked at Heidi, who stood there in total shock at what she'd inadvertently done. I tried to comfort her with a quick report about my health. "I'm fine, Heidi. I don't feel a thing." I was telling the truth because when a person is numb, there is no feeling. What happened next sent Heidi running into the house. I took my fingers off the knot and blood spurted out of the laceration like a fountain. It must have been an awful thing to see. It's no wonder that my loving daughter ran inside. However, I was left wondering if I was consigned to die alone out in the yard. Thirty seconds later I realized she had not abandoned me. No, she had hurried inside to get her mama.

Annie showed up with a towel to mop up "the spill" from the divot in my face. After sending Heidi across the street to stay with a friend, Annie loaded me into the car, and we headed to the emergency room for stitches. Later that evening I pulled Heidi into my lap. I could tell she felt guilty. She leaned against my chest, and I hugged her. I offered my best attempt at consoling her worried heart. "Heidi, I won't mind having the scar that will be there after this cut heals."

She seemed puzzled at my statement. "You won't? Why's that, Dad?"

"Because I can tell people I spent time with my kids and I have a scar to prove it!"

Her smile told me she understood. Then I made another statement that I prayed she would someday fully understand and that she would remember for the rest of her life. "I love you very much, Heidi, but there's Someone else who loves you even more than I do. And He has scars to prove it too." I then talked to her about the scars on Jesus' hands and feet that were put there when He was crucified on the cross in our place as a sacrifice for our sins. "His scars are not like the scar I'll have because my scar was put there because of an accident with a golf club. Jesus' scars are there because He accepted them on purpose. He chose to receive them when He didn't deserve them so we wouldn't have to be punished for our sin. For that reason, we owe Him everything."

Heidi is now grown and, thankfully, she does understand and embrace the meaning of the scars Christ bore for her. And she's passing on that wisdom to her children. From time to time she comments on the permanent slice she inadvertently put in my golf game and what she learned from it. I still reassure her that I'm proud of it. I also tell her that every time I stand at the mirror to shave I remember how much I love her.

As for the battle-marked, ten-point buck, oh how I wish I would have taken it to a taxidermist and had a head mount done, scar and all. Unfortunately, the rack is all that remains. But when I see it, I can't help but recall the mark it wore on its hide. This is a reminder of what it means to wear proof on the outside of the love that lies within.

18

The Great Surprise

I looked at the watch on my wrist and whispered, "Seven-twenty. They should be here in about ten minutes." On a couple of other mornings I'd observed a herd of deer enter the lower end of the field I was hunting around 7:30, but each time they were too far away and out of range for my muzzle loader. Choosing to set up closer to that spot and on the ground under a wide-trunk oak, I closed the gap a good 75 yards on where I thought they would show up. If they did, the range for the weighty .50 caliber bullet would be a manageable 80 to 90 yards.

Though they were a little late, five females appeared. One-by-one they stepped into the open and began browsing. They had no idea I was watching as they spread out and fed. When their eyes were focused on searching for edible grasses, I slowly raised the heavy-barreled gun to my knee. I studied the group. There were two mothers, two youngsters, and a doe that appeared to be "dry," that is, old enough to be a mom but without an offspring. She would be my choice since, I admit, I can be a softie when it comes to separating moms and kids.

I had my eye on the fawnless doe, but she seemed to deliberately keep the others between us. I wondered if she possessed some sort of special sense that she was being considered as a candidate for freezer wrap. Finally she meandered away from the foursome. Now all she had to do was turn broadside and I'd have my bead on her. That positioning seemed to take another forever, but at last it was time to pull the hammer back and drop it on the cap.

When the charge exploded, the area beneath the oak became a container of smoke so thick I had to quickly crawl out to the side a couple of feet just to get a reading on how many deer were running toward the woods. Were there four...or five? Their departure happened so fast I couldn't tell.

When the breeze finally carried the smoke wall away, I stood up and dug for my binoculars. While scanning the area where the deer had been feeding, I saw a tuft of white fur.

"Aha! One down!" I said. I confess it felt good to have a plan, stick with it, and watch it work out successfully. Since there was no one else around, I engaged in a little self-congratulating as I gathered up my backpack and headed across the field to check out the reward of my well-schemed hunt. Yes, even the words "Yoo da man!" came tumbling out of my mouth. I grinned, not knowing my gloating was going to be short-lived.

When I got a mere 12 or so feet from the downed doe, she suddenly stood up, looked at me, turned her head toward the woods where her friends had gone, and bolted away. It was like she'd been shot out of a giant slingshot! So much for my assumption that she'd quickly expired as a result of a well-placed shot.

And what did I do in that moment? Nothing. Why? Because when I'd seen her through the binoculars looking lifeless, I'd decided she was dead. Because of that errant judgment, I hadn't reloaded. Was that a costly decision? Yep. And it wasn't laziness or an attempt to conserve powder and bullets. Nope. It was simply a bad call on my part. I should have approached the doe ready to react with a deal-closing shot if necessary.

As I stood there feeling the pain of being snookered by a female, I listened hard. I was hoping to hear a crashing sound in the dry leaves where she had escaped. You know, the audible evidence that would tell me her "dead run" was just that. Unfortunately, no sound like that happened. With that, I knew the rest of the morning would be spent back at the cabin waiting a couple of hours and then coming back to search for a blood trail.

The problem with the waiting was the replaying of the scene that went on in my head. There was all the kicking my own behind that I had to endure for being so careless. How could I have failed to reload the muzzle loader after the shot? I *always* did—but not that day.

Almost three hours passed before I headed back to the field to track the wounded doe. I didn't find any red stuff until I entered the woods. And then the drops were few and far between. With each passing minute my dejection sunk lower and lower. I was caught in the mire of regret. When the trail completely stopped, I sighed deep and faced the defeat. I'd invested nearly four hours in the search and was finally convinced my shot had not mortally wounded the doe. Instead, it obviously just addled her for a few minutes—just enough time to allow me to show up so I could learn a hard lesson.

If I had a dollar for every time the sight of that doe standing up within a few feet of me has played in my noggin, I'd be a wealthy man. Each time it rewinds and rolls again, I feel the sting of my blunder. But there is at least one redeemable thought that came to me during one of the replays—a comparison that has helped heal the wound of the experience. It has to do with my reaction to the resurrection that took place in the field that morning and the reaction of those who discovered another resurrection that took place more than 2000 years ago.

That doe looked very dead when I walked up to it. She was lying there completely motionless, seemingly ready for my post-kill surgery. In my mind's eye I can still see that flash of a slight flinch in her side when I got close—just before she instantly, in one motion, rose to her feet and looked right at me.

I do believe if there had been a recording of my face when that critter bolted upright, I'd be a doubly rich man. I could have sold the footage to any number of ad agencies who were searching for a model of utter surprise for some commercial. I'm sure my jaw dropped, my brow tensed, and my head went forward. I may have even gasped an exasperated, "What? Hey! Where you goin', girl?" as the doe sped away.

When Jesus was crucified by the Romans, the apostle Peter knew his Lord and friend was dead. Peter had no cause to believe otherwise. And unlike the doe that was only addled, Jesus had physically died and was even placed in a tomb. When Mary went to the resting place of Jesus' body early on the first day of the week while it was still dark, she saw the stone in front of the opening had been rolled away. She ran to Simon Peter and John to report that Jesus' body had been taken, and she didn't know where they had carried it.

Hearing Mary's announcement, the two men took off running to the gravesite. The more fleet-footed John won the race and peered inside the tomb, but he didn't go in. No doubt his face showed amazement and maybe even bewilderment as he surveyed the inside and surrounding area.

But Peter, in typical fashion, didn't stop at the door. He boldly shot right by John and entered the tomb to verify firsthand that Mary's report was accurate. John then followed him inside, and they found that the tomb did not contain a body. Only the grave clothes were in there.

Here's my point. Even though my look of surprise over the doe that seemingly came back to life might be a weak comparison, I believe that experience gave me a small glimpse at what astonishment must have been evident on Peter and John's faces when they realized their Master had risen from the dead. Can you imagine?

I sincerely wish that when I reach the other side and am in that place where time is no longer a concern, that God, who is not bound by time, will take me back to that moment. I would love to see the expressions of total awe that had to be visible on the disciples' faces as a result of such a great surprise. Yes, my look of surprise and theirs is different in that mine was spoiled by the knowledge of failure. Their faces, on the other hand, were most assuredly brightened with joy, victory, relief, and blessed hope that never disappointed them once they realized what had happened. And this is true for everyone who chooses to believe in and accept Jesus as their Savior and Lord!

19

The Cry

By the time the long summer was over and bow season arrived in late September, I was so pumped about going out the first day that I seriously considered going to my stand the night before and sleeping in it until daybreak. I decided to keep out of temptation's path by sleeping at home, but I've never missed being in the woods as badly as I did that year. So when the four o'clock buzzer woke me the next morning, it was a welcome sound.

My pack was filled with all the stuff I usually carry. I had things like my trusty mesh, see-through head net that would keep the pesky gnats off my face. I had my camo-patterned, rubber-studded gloves that helped me hold onto my bow during a shot. I carried my little pair of binoculars that weren't that impressive but very dependable. Also I had my old, dog-eared tiny New Testament that would help me be more spiritually industrious while waiting in the tree stand. There were several other well-used items that had been in the pack since the season before that I felt like I couldn't do without too. But that wasn't all. There was something new in the mix.

I had watched yet another hunting video prior to the beginning of the season. This one featured a call that simulates the voice of a fawn. The guys who demonstrated it on camera nearly got ran over by one particular doe that responded to the cry of "her" little one. I was amazed at the effectiveness of the device and promptly went to the sporting goods store in our area and picked one up. The recording that came with it made it easy to learn to use. I couldn't wait to give it a try during early bow season.

I candidly admit that if a doe answered the call because she believed it was from a scared or threatened fawn, I had no plans of taking her. I simply have yet to get that hungry. I determined long ago that I would not knowingly take a mama from her young child. There've been a few times when I inadvertently broke that self-imposed rule, and it always left me with an empty feeling. For the most part though, I've been faithful to it. Now, if times got tough enough and my family desperately needed the meat, I wouldn't hesitate to break this policy. But for now my plan for using the call was more for the interest of seeing in real life the kind of female behavior I'd watched on the video.

When ten o'clock came that morning and no four-legged critter had wandered by my stand, I decided it was time to give the fawn call a try. The wind was up just a little, and I wasn't totally sure how far the sound would reach so I gave it a couple of unreserved blows. The piercing tone seemed to cut through the surrounding area like a crossbow dart. It was a strange mixture of sound, surprisingly loud yet tenderly soft. Just to be sure, I gave the call a couple more tries before putting it into my shirt pocket.

A minute, maybe two, went by while I carefully watched my surroundings. I was set up in a climber along a line of trees at a field that was not more than 60 yards wide. With no immediate response to the call, I got it out and gave it two more blows. Again the sound punctured the morning air.

Before I could drop the plastic call back into my pocket, I saw movement to my left, in the woods on the other side of the field. All at once, like a fireman running into a burning house looking for occupants, a doe shot into the open and stopped ten yards or so from the edge of the timber. She looked both ways for a few seconds before starting a full bouncing run across the field, all the while turning her head in search of a youngster.

It was an amazing and heartwarming thing to watch as this doe responded with its motherly instincts. Looking confused and worried as she ran under my stand (not knowing she was being watched), she went about 20 yards into the woods behind me and stopped. I could almost hear her panting as she turned from one side to the other, searching for a fawn. Finally the anxious doe ran deeper into the woods and disappeared. I thought about tooting on the call again, but didn't have the heart to add more panic to an already frazzled mother.

Since that unforgettable day, I have found two other uses for the call. The sound of a fawn in distress is a real enticement for a hungry coyote. (That also explains why the doe was so urgent in her mission to find the fawn.)

The call also makes an excellent tool for teaching children an important spiritual truth.

Our daughter, Heidi, was driving with her two girls across the county to our house. I was finishing up organizing some boxes of hunting gear. I found the fawn call and thought about how fun it might be for the little human children to hear the voice of a youngster from the animal kingdom. When they arrived and got out of the car, I met them with call in hand. "Wanna hear what a baby deer sounds like when it cries out to its mama?" I asked.

The two little girls humored their granddad and gave a nod. I blew the high-pitched call, and their eyes widened. They reached out their hands simultaneously, wanting to give the call a try. We stood in the driveway, and for three or four minutes they took turns making the unique sound of a fawn. They were intrigued just like I'd hoped they would be.

We finally went inside. Before we had lunch, I called Lily and Josie into the den. "Hey, girls," I said, "let me tell you what the fawn is saying when it makes the sound this call makes." My two little students were all ears.

I blew the call softly. "Come find me, Mama!" I said afterward. I blew it again. "I'm lost, Mama! Come find me!"

Their reaction was sweet as they listened. I continued. "When a fawn is in trouble, the cry gets louder and more serious, like this!" I gave the call a very strong, sharp blow. The resulting distressed sound made the girls' eyes fill with concern, especially when I said, "Something's trying to hurt me, Mama! Come quick! Please!"

"What would make a fawn so afraid, Papa?" one of them asked.

"Big, bad, hungry coyotes. Wolves are a threat to them too. Even huge eagles have been known to attack fawns. But don't forget, the best defense a little deer has is its cry. When it cries out, its mama will come running and fight whatever is trying to hurt her baby."

There was relief on my grandgirls' faces when they realized that the little deer's cry would bring help. That's when I took the chance to tell them one of the most important lessons they would ever learn from God's great outdoors.

"Lily and Josie, when you were born—when you came into this world—the first thing we heard out of your mouths was a cry. In fact, we weren't happy until we heard you cry right after you were born. The sound told everyone in the room that you were alive and well. Your cry is special to your mom and dad and to me and your Dee Dee (Grandma Annie). When we hear it, we come running. When you fall and scrape your skin and cry, whoever is around shows up. Why? Because we love you, and we want to help you."

Lily chimed in. "Yes, and I like it when you or Dee Dee put the Elmo Band-Aid on me."

Little Josie added, "And I want the purple one!"

I could tell they were engaged in the conversation, so I went on. "And, girls, do you know who else hears your cry?"

Two little voices answered at the same time: "Who, Papa?"

"God loves the sound of your cries."

"Really?" Their expressions turned curious.

"He sure does. There are a couple of verses in Psalm 145 in the Bible that I want you to hear." I picked up the Scriptures from the table and opened to verses 18 and 19 in the chapter. "The LORD is near to all who call upon Him, to all who call upon Him in truth. He will fulfill the desire of those who fear Him; He will also hear their cry and will save them."

One more time I gave a soft blow on the fawn call and added, "Just like the mama deer hurries to her little baby when she hears its cry, just like we run to you when we hear you cry, our Father in heaven comes to us when He hears us call out to Him. Don't ever be afraid to cry out to God whenever you need Him. And always believe these verses in His Word are true because they are! He will be here for you. You can count on it!"

The girls took in every word I said. I consider this one of the most special moments I'll ever spend with them. I hope that when they come to times when they need God's presence, for whatever reason, they'll remember the fawn call. I pray it will encourage them to value their own ability to cry out for help.

And I hope it will do that for you too. The next time you are deer hunting and hear a fawn call out to its mama, I pray you will be reminded that your cry is important to God too.

20

The Line on the Wall

As a professional musician and songwriter, when I hear a story that tugs at my heartstrings, my normal reaction is to find a way to create a lyric around it. That's exactly what happened when my friend and fellow musician Pastor Mark Grayless shared an account with me a few years ago about a husband who was, like the two of us, a hunter.

The lyrical tribute to this husband is not just about him. His wife, who is now a widow, is also a main character in the song:

The Line on the Wall

It's been about a year since he's been gone
She's been doing good with moving on with her life
She's been to the hardware store
She started painting that back room, it needed to be
  done
It was looking brand-new, she was working all alone
That's when she saw it—that line on the wall by the
  door

She never cared for that scar where his old
  Winchester stood

155

He'd always lean it there when he came home
    from the woods
But the sight of it now sends her walking back
    through the years
She remembers the light in his eyes when he'd
    pick up that old gun
And as he'd leave for the hills before the rising sun
She can still hear him whisper, "Babe, you're my
    favorite dear!"

Now she remembers all of the times
She painted over that line
And she wondered if he'd ever change at all
But today she'll leave that line on the wall

As she painted around that mark he made
She thought of all the times she felt so afraid
When he'd leave with that gun, would he come
    home again?
But today she's so glad that in all of their years
She never said a word about her fears
And what she'd give right now to hear him come
    walking in

She remembers all of the times
She painted over that line
And she wondered if he'd ever change at all
But today she'll leave that line on the wall[8]

Since the writing of the lyric, whenever I come home from a hunt and put my gear away, the couple in that story often comes to mind. While I'm not guilty of leaning my rifle against a wall in a back room and leaving a scar on the paint that would challenge my wife's patience, there are other ways I might make a scratch that needs some necessary attention.

For example, there are mornings when I arrive later than I want at a parking spot at the edge of the woods I'll be hunting. I quickly exit the truck, check the sky for lightness, and note that sunrise is fewer minutes away than would allow me to sneak to my stand in predawn darkness unseen by the local deer herd. To hurry things up, instead of using a few extra seconds to get out of my street clothes and change into my hunting duds like I usually do, I take a shortcut and throw my camo coveralls on top of my good clothes.

This tactic is not a bad one when using a firearm and the deer aren't close enough to smell the unnatural odor of laundry detergent and dryer sheets that escapes from the garments under my coveralls. However, wearing clothes from my closet is not a good thing if I manage to connect with a deer. Then I have to engage in the messy task of field dressing. Unfortunately, in the excitement of my success, I seem to always forget what I'm wearing—until I get home. That's when Annie finds the red stains of my blunder. They're usually located on the ends of my sleeves or the cuffs of my pants.

My propensity for bloodying my nice clothes wouldn't be a problem for Annie if I knew how to do laundry. But before you marvel at my domestic ineptness, there is a good reason I'm not skilled in that area. Annie explains it best when she tells others about our arrangement, one that has worked well for us throughout our married life. The way she states it is simply, "Steve and I have an agreement. I don't do faxes, and he doesn't do laundry!"

Annie readily admits that when it comes to using modern electronic technology, she'd rather have a root canal in an endodontist's chair. And I have accepted the fact that even though my wife is a brilliant woman who has written many books while sitting at a computer, she despises the gadgetry. Word processing is just about all she can tolerate. I'm well aware that if I wanted to push her over the line emotionally, all I have to do is ask her to fax something for me. She'd break out in a cold sweat, her fingers would go numb, and her eyes would get a scary, blank look. And the funny thing is that she knows she could generate those same reactions in me by asking me to do a load of laundry.

In the handful of instances I've had to wash our clothes because Annie wasn't there to do it, I've had to track her down by phone (or call our daughter or my mother) and ask again how to operate the machine. For some reason, the process doesn't stick in my head. Plus I have to ask again, "Just what constitutes the division between darks and lights? Where does the soap go? And is one lid full of detergent all that is needed for a load? Wouldn't two be better?"

I suppose if I did laundry more often I'd learn what buttons to push and remember all the details of the process. Thankfully, however, my sweet wife seems content to be the laundry queen at our house. And if Annie used electronic technology more often, she would eventually not feel so squeamish when she walks by the fax machine. But I have happily resolved to be the "fax and e-mail" king in our home office. While these little quirks in our personalities might drive other couples to quarrels, Annie and I choose to accept and even laugh at them.

I can't help but believe that the husband and wife featured in the "Line on the Wall" lyric had a similar relationship. The reason I think this is found in the imagery of her meticulously painting around the line and intentionally preserving the evidence of her late hunter's presence in her life. Obviously he wasn't a perfect husband, but it's safe to assume he did enough things right as a mate to cause her to sorely miss him after he was gone. Maybe he accomplished this amazing feat by being willing to paint around the scratches, so to speak, that she sometimes made in the wall of their marriage.

Perhaps, for example, he didn't get upset when she forgot to do subtraction in their checkbook, or he was patient with her when she lost her cell phone—again, or failed to give him a message because she was distracted by tending to their children. There's no way to know for sure how he might have returned the patience she displayed for his rifle line on the wall, but he surely did. Otherwise she probably would have put two coats of paint over that ugly scar. Instead, because he apparently left behind a legacy of kindheartedness, she let the line remain as a visible reminder of a good man.

As a husband who loves and lives to hunt, I sincerely hope that if it happens that I am the first to leave the woods of life and enter the fields of eternity, I will consider it my greatest trophy if I'm as missed by Annie as the hunter in "The Line on the Wall" is missed by his wife. May it be so.

> The memory of the righteous is blessed, but the name of the wicked will rot (Proverbs 10:7).

Notes

CHAPTER 3: THE ARROW AND THE BOW

1. Words and music by S. Chapman. © 1987 Shepherds Fold Music. Administered by EMI Christian Music Publishing. All rights reserved. Used by permission.

CHAPTER 4: THE DOING OF THIS THING

2. Words and music by Steve Chapman, Times & Seasons Music/BMI. Used by permission.

CHAPTER 5: HE'S COMIN', DADDY

3. Steve & Annie Chapman, *Gifts Your Kids Can't Break* (Minneapolis, MN: Bethany House Publishers, 1991), p. 51. Used by permission.

CHAPTER 6: THE VAPOR

4. Words and music by S. Chapman. © 1987 Shepherds Fold Music/Dawn Treader Music. Administered by EMI Christian Music Publishing. All rights reserved. Used by permission.

CHAPTER 11: SUNRISE

5. Words and music by S. Chapman, Times & Seasons Music/BMI. Used by permission.

CHAPTER 14: LOST AND FOUND

6. Words and music by S. Chapman, Times & Seasons Music/BMI. Used by permission.

CHAPTER 17: SCARS OF LOVE

7. Words by S. Chapman, Times & Seasons Music/BMI/2011. Used by permission.

CHAPTER 20: THE LINE ON THE WALL

8. Words by Steve Chapman & Mark Grayless, "The Line on the Wall," Times & Seasons Music/BMI/2007. Used by permission.

Discography

The song lyrics found in these pages are from the following recorded projects:

"Man to Man"
From *Tools for the Trade,* Steve & Annie Chapman
S&A Family, Inc., SACD-7000

"The Arrow and the Bow"
From *The Miles,* Steve & Annie Chapman
S&A Family, Inc., SACD-2803

"Seasons of a Man"
From *Tools for the Trade,* Steve & Annie Chapman
S&A Family, Inc., SACD-7000

"Reachable"
From *Family Favorites,* Steve & Annie Chapman
S&A Family, Inc., SACD-105

"The Key"
From *Family Favorites,* Steve & Annie Chapman
S&A Family, Inc., SACD-105

~

For a list of available music and books or
for more information about the Chapmans,
please visit their website:

www.steveandanniechapman.com

or write to:

S&A Family
PO Box 337
Pleasant View, TN 37146

About the Author

Proudly claiming West Virginia as his home state, Steve Chapman grew up as the son of a preacher. He met his wife, Annie, in junior high school in 1963. In March of 1975, they married after dating a few months and settled in Nashville, Tennessee. There they have raised their son and daughter, Nathan and Heidi.

Steve is president of S&A Family, Inc., an organization formed to oversee the production of the Chapmans' recorded music. They have had "family life" as the theme of their lyrics since they began singing together in 1980. As Dove Award-winning artists, their schedule sends them to over 100 cities a year to present a concert that features songs from over 15 recorded projects.

Steve's love of hunting began in his early teens on a weekend when one of his dad's church members invited him to tag along on an October squirrel hunt. Archery is his first choice for use in the field, followed by muzzle loader, and then pistol or rifle. To date, according to Steve's calculations, he has entered the woods before daylight on well over a thousand mornings. He says he hopes for just as many more.

More Great Harvest House Books for Sportsmen

—— BY STEVE CHAPMAN ——

Another Look at Life from a Deer Stand

A Look at Life from a Deer Stand Devotional

A Look at Life from the Riverbank

365 Things Every Hunter Should Know

Great Hunting Stories

The Hunter's Cookbook

The Hunter's Devotional

My Dream Hunt in Alaska

A Sportsman's Call

Stories from the Deer Stand

The Tales Hunters Tell

With Dad on a Deer Stand

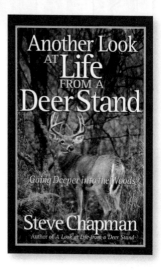

ANOTHER LOOK AT LIFE FROM A DEER STAND

Steve Chapman shares even more lessons of life and faith learned on the hunt. With humorous and insightful writing, Scriptures, song lyrics, and lots of tales from the woods, Steve trains your eye on wisdom such as this:

- It's not too late to sow love in the lives of others.
- Errors on the hunt offer answers for life at home.
- Changing one's course can lead to singing a new song.

Hunters, outdoorsmen, and anyone who enjoys devotional stories and Steve's own pencil sketches will look forward to time spent following the trail of truth to the heart of the Creator.

A LOOK AT LIFE FROM A DEER STAND DEVOTIONAL

Steve Chapman has a gift for gleaning faith lessons from the glories of creation. This pocket-sized gathering of devotions, handsomely bound in a soft, suede-like cover, invites you to join in the thrill of the pursuit, the celebration of nature, and the enjoyment of God's presence.

Each devotion begins with the inspiration of a Scripture verse and closes with the stillness of a prayer. You'll be excited by the application of biblical wisdom, delighted by the humor, caught up in the adventure of hunting, and intrigued by the exploration of God's character.

An ideal gift for Steve Chapman fans, hunters, outdoor enthusiasts, and anyone who wants to take aim at spiritual growth.

THE HUNTER'S COOKBOOK
More than 200 easy and delicious recipes!

Expert hunter Steve Chapman, and his wife, Annie, an experienced wild game cook, team up to bring you tasty ways to prepare the bounty God provides. From bear to boar, from deer to duck, from trout to turtle, you'll discover mouth-watering recipes that make dinner a time to celebrate, including:

- Easy Venison Meatloaf
- Broiled Fish Parmesan
- Elk Roast
- Pan-fried Duck Breast Nuggets

- Red Snapper Jubilee
- Venison Stroganoff
- Wild Turkey Crock-Pot Supper

Along with easy-to-follow recipes for main courses, side dishes, and desserts, you'll find Steve's enjoyable family-oriented hunting and fishing stories—perfect for sharing at the table. The delicious recipes and exciting tales create a one-of-a-kind cookbook that will have your family clamoring for more and wanting to spend active time together outdoors.

To learn more about Harvest House books and
to read sample chapters, visit our website:

www.harvesthousepublishers.com

HARVEST HOUSE PUBLISHERS
EUGENE, OREGON